a month in
RECIPES FROM THE HEART OF MOROCCO
MARRAKESH

hardie grant books

MELBOURNE · LONDON

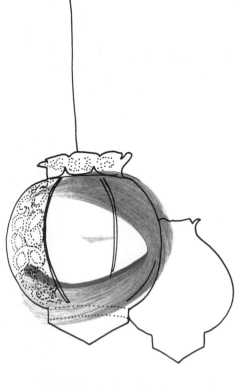

**First published in hardback in 2011 by
Hardie Grant Books
This paperback edition published in 2012**

Hardie Grant Books (UK)
Dudley House, North Suite
34–35 Southampton Street
London WC2E 7HF
www.hardiegrant.co.uk

Hardie Grant Books (Australia)
Ground Floor, Building 1
658 Church Street
Melbourne, VIC 3121
www.hardiegrant.com.au

A copy of the British Library Cataloguing-in-
Publication data is available from the British Library.

ISBN: 978-1-74270-412-8

Design: Interstate Associates
Editor: Camilla Davis
Indexer: Marian Anderson
Proofreaders: Jasmine Parker and Holly O'Neill
Colour reproduction: MDP

**Printed and bound in China
by C&C Offset Printing**

1 3 5 7 9 10 8 6 4 2

To both our beloved parents,
Jean & Alec and Eric & Jean

Andy & David
x

Contents

I first went to Marrakesh
   twenty years ago.
   I remember staying
in a cheap and cheerful hotel
   just off the Djemaa el Fna square,
   long before the rise of the hundreds
   of restored riads that have now
been turned into designer hotels.

Marrakesh

On my first trip to Marrakesh, I was unable to sleep because of the cloying heat in my tiny room and the wail of the muezzin from the nearby Koutoubia Mosque, calling the faithful to prayer. It was also nigh impossible to walk alone in the city without being hassled by aggressive gangs of locals, in search of dirhams in return for the dubious pleasure of escorting you through the meandering streets of the nearby souks. Mercifully the progressive King Mohammed VI has banned such blatant touting today, so it's a real joy to wander around the labyrinthine medina again.

For the past ten years, I've been going to my best friend Trevor Hopkins' riad on an annual basis. We do little but explore the food markets and go to favourite shops and stalls in the souks to buy mad Moroccan kitchen utensils, colourful bowls and large unwieldy earthenware tagines that always seem to break on the trip home.

Like any holiday experiences, it gets tiring eating out every night so it's always a pleasure to cook at home for family and friends. I spend most of my mornings at the Mellah Market buying fresh ingredients and try to make it to the Beldi Country Club just outside the city in the afternoon, where everyone's ensconced around the pool drinking copious amounts of the quaffable local rosé wine. Back at the riad, there's just time to prepare all the salads and tagines for our impromptu dinner parties, which always end in rowdy games of Scrabble played by an open fire.

Despite all the changes that tourism has brought to this timeless city (with all sorts of trendy hotels, restaurants and bars opening on every street corner), it's the familiarity and integrity of its ancient markets – where you still choose your live chicken for the pot or simply take a *tangia* (an amphora-shaped earthenware pot) filled with meat, vegetables and spices to the local *farnatchi* (oven) to be slow-cooked in charcoal embers – that continues to excite me about Marrakesh. Joining the locals, who cook fresh dishes based on seasonal ingredients on a daily basis, I still feel that I've only just begun to discover the secrets of this inspirational and vibrant cuisine in the recipes created in this book.

Today, I've even got used to the regular croak of the muezzin and braying of the donkeys in the tortuous alleys, and always sleep surprisingly well.

Breakfasts

Like any hard-working nation, they take breakfast very seriously in Morocco. Workers who have been in the fields since dawn can be seen slurping bowls of hearty pulse soups or crushing boiled eggs and spicy olives onto freshly baked bread. In the towns and cities, market stalls offer up still-warm pancakes drizzled with honey, and locals watch the world go by in cafes, sipping on copious amounts of sickly sweet mint tea or dunking pastries into strong black coffee.

Serves 2
- 4 sheets warkha pastry or 8 sheets filo pastry
- olive oil, for brushing or frying
- 1 teaspoon ground cinnamon
- 4 teaspoons thick Greek-style yoghurt
- amlou (see page 264)

To serve
- ground cinnamon, for dusting
- 4 teaspoons clear runny honey

Amlou & Yoghurt Bistilla

In North Africa, they use a thin, delicate and transparent pastry called warkha, made by dabbing small amounts of an elastic dough onto an upturned saucepan placed over a pot of hot water. The resultant pastry sheet is peeled off after a few minutes. It makes a wonderful wrap for briouat or brik pastries, with savoury or sweet fillings. Warkha is hard to make at home, but can be bought from specialist delis and supermarkets or substituted with filo pastry. Depending on the size of the pastry sheets you buy, you might need more sheets than stated in the recipes. You can either bake or fry the warkha.

If you use filo pastry instead, simply fry it briefly in a little olive oil until golden.

Preheat the oven to 200°C (400°F). Cut the warkha pastry into twelve 10cm (4in) circles. Place the circles on a baking tray, brush with olive oil and sprinkle with cinnamon. Bake the warkha for about 5 minutes until crisp. Remove from the oven and allow to cool on the tray.

If frying, heat the olive oil over a medium heat and shallow-fry the warkha in batches if necessary. Transfer to a waiting plate lined with kitchen paper.

To assemble, place a circle of warkha on a plate and smear with yoghurt and amlou. Repeat this process with four more pastry circles, then top with a final circle of warkha. Make a second plate using the remaining ingredients.

Sprinkle with cinnamon, drizzle with honey and serve immediately.

Beghrir with Honey

These semolina pancakes are a breakfast staple in Marrakesh; honeycombed on one side, they are perfect for absorbing honey and melted butter.

Place the yeast, sugar and a pinch of salt in a bowl with 100ml warm water. Mix well and leave in a warm place for 15 minutes.

Beat the eggs in a bowl. Add the milk and 150ml (5fl oz) cold water, and whisk until combined.

Place the semolina, flour and a pinch of salt in a large bowl and mix well. Make a well in the middle and slowly add the egg mixture, stirring constantly with a wooden spoon until well blended. Add the yeast mixture and stir until well combined. Continue to beat for about 5 minutes until the mixture is light and runny, adding a little more water if the mixture seems too thick. Cover with a tea towel and rest for 1–2 hours.

Heat a large cast iron or heavy based frying pan, lightly oiled with vegetable oil, over medium heat. Pour a ladle of the pancake batter into the pan and smooth into a circle with the back of a spoon. Cook until the surface is filled with little bubbles or holes. Transfer to a plate and repeat the process with the remaining batter.

Serve pancakes, honeycombed side up, with melted butter and honey. Sliced melon or other seasonal fruit can also be added.

Serves 4 (makes 10 pancakes)
- 15g (½oz) dried yeast
- 1 teaspoon sugar
- salt
- 100ml (3½fl oz/approx ½ cup) warm water, plus 150ml (5fl oz/ approx ⅔ cup) cold water
- 2 eggs
- 150ml (5fl oz/approx ⅔ cup) milk
- 250g (9oz/1½ cups) semolina
- 250g (9oz/1⅔ cups) plain (all-purpose) flour
- vegetable oil, for frying

To serve
- melted butter
- clear runny honey

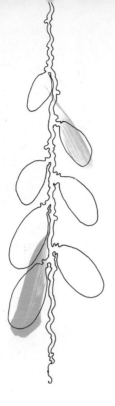

Date & Almond Compote with Yoghurt & Sweet Warkha Pastry

For the Date & Almond Compote, place all the ingredients in a saucepan. Add the water and simmer over a low heat, stirring occasionally. Add a little extra water if the mixture is too dry. Simmer for about 20–30 minutes until mixture thickens to a soft and sticky consistency. Allow to cool before using. Remove bay leaves and allow to cool.

Preheat the oven to 200°C (400°F). Place the sheets of warkha on a baking tray, brush with olive oil and sprinkle with brown sugar and cinnamon. Bake for about 5 minutes or until crisp. Remove from oven and allow to cool.

Filo pastry can be used instead of warkha. Simply fry briefly in a little olive oil until golden, and remove to a plate lined with kitchen paper.

Combine the yoghurt, lemon juice and zest in a bowl and mix well. To assemble, place a layer of Date & Almond Compote in six small glasses. Add a layer of Yoghurt Filling to each glass and then top with a generous dollop of compote.

Cut the warkha pastry into large shards and place in the top of each glass. Sprinkle with icing sugar and serve.

Serves 4
- 4 sheets warkha pastry or 8 sheets filo pastry
- 1 tablespoon extra-virgin olive oil, for brushing
- 1 tablespoon brown sugar
- 1 teaspoon ground cinnamon

Date & Almond Compote
- 200g (7oz/approx 1 cup) pitted dates
- 80g (3oz/approx 1 cup) almonds, chopped
- 2 fresh bay leaves
- ½ teaspoon dried thyme
- a few dried rose petals
- 1 tablespoon caster (superfine) sugar
- 300ml (10fl oz/approx 1⅕ cup) cold water

Yoghurt Filling
- 400g (14oz/1⅗ cup) thick Greek-style yoghurt
- juice and zest of ½ lemon

To serve
- icing (confectioner's) sugar

Away from the Medina, it's worth visiting Gueliz, the New Town built by the French in the early 20th century. Stroll around its wide avenues filled with pavement cafes, perfect for breakfast Croque Monsieur and café au lait; explore the antique and leather goods shops; eat classic steak frites; and salade Nicoise at old-fashioned brasseries and visit the Hotel Toulousain in a little courtyard off the Rue Tarik Ben Ziad Gueliz. This atmospheric hotel, built by a Frenchman from Toulouse, was a favourite of beat writer William Burroughs and is next door to the lively Café Du Livre, which sells bargain second-hand books and homemade cakes.

ELECTRICITE

Art Galleries

Shoe Shines Galore

Hidden Nightclubs

Café au lait

Palm Trees

Colonial Architecture

Patisserie

Hivernage

Rue de la Liberté

Beat Poet Inspiration

HOTEL TOULOUSAIN

Serves 4–6
- 500g (1lb 2oz/2½ cups) couscous
- cold water
- 2 tablespoons extra-virgin olive oil
- ½ teaspoon ground cinnamon
- salt
- cold water
- 180g (6oz/approx 1½ sticks) butter

To serve
- icing (confectioner's) sugar
- cinnamon
- cold milk

Seffa

This is the purest version of seffa, where perfectly cooked couscous is simply served with cinnamon, icing sugar and bowls of cold milk. It is a wonderful dish if you are feeling poorly. I use a couscoussier in these recipes, but if you don't have one simply use a steamer.

Place the couscous in a bowl and cover with cold water. With your hands, mix well and then drain immediately using a fine sieve. To break up any lumps, rub the grains together with your hands, letting them fall back into the bowl. Leave for 10 minutes.

Add the olive oil, ground cinnamon, a pinch of salt and about 100ml (3½ fl oz) cold water to the couscous. Mix well with your hands until liquid is absorbed.

Fill the bottom part of a couscoussier three-quarters full with water, bring to the boil and then add the couscous into the top part. Cover with the lid and steam for 30 minutes. Remove from the heat and transfer the couscous to a large bowl.

Allow to cool then mix in 60g (2oz) butter with your hands and combine well with the couscous grains. Then slowly add about 300ml (10fl oz) cold water and combine. Return the couscous to the top part of couscoussier and steam for a further 20 minutes.

Remove from the heat and transfer the couscous back to the large bowl. Allow to cool then add another 60g (2oz) butter and mix again with your hands. Return the couscous to the top part of couscoussier and steam for a further 20 minutes until the grains are swollen and soft.

Remove from the heat and transfer the couscous back to the large bowl. Allow to cool then add a final 60g (2oz) butter and mix until well combined using your hands. Spoon the couscous onto a serving plate and mould into a small dome shape. Sprinkle with icing sugar and cinnamon, and serve with bowls of cold milk.

Note For a quick alternative you can use 'instant' couscous – just follow instructions on the packet.

Seffa with Stewed Fruits

Serves 4-6

- 250g (9oz/2½ cups) apples, cored and roughly chopped
- 100g (3½oz/1¼ cups) dried apricots, roughly chopped
- 100g (3½oz/ 1¼ cups) prunes, stoned and roughly chopped
- 100g (3½oz/⅔ cup) raisins
- 100g (3½oz/1 cup) pistachios, shelled and roughly chopped
- ½ teaspoon saffron threads
- cold water
- seffa (see page 10)

To serve
- clear runny honey
- cinnamon

For the stewed fruits, place the apple, dried fruits, pistachios and saffron threads in a large saucepan. Add about 200ml (7fl oz) cold water and simmer over a low heat. Stir occasionally and add a little extra water if the mixture is too dry. Simmer for about 20-30 minutes or until the fruit is cooked and the mixture thickens to a soft and sticky consistency. Set aside to cool. Meanwhile, make the Seffa.

To assemble, spoon the stewed fruits over the couscous. Drizzle with honey, dust with cinnamon and serve.

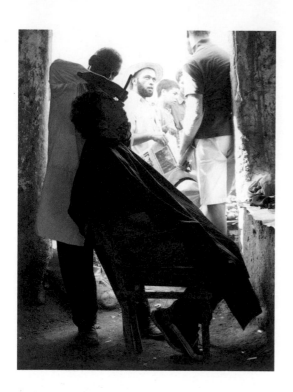

I'd always wanted an
  authentic Moroccan shaving
experience and nothing can
  beat the one I had at Sidei ⋀⋀⋀⋀
    Sidi Abdallah Ghiat,
  ten miles south of Marrakesh.
  There's a Sunday morning
    Berber market that's
  rimmed by cramped, cave-like
    mud and wattle rooms
  where barbers ply their trade.

         I sat on the floor, waiting my turn
    with a complementary glass of sweet
      mint tea as a persistent Berber
    tried to sell me a dozen or so
                  silver bracelets.

         It was a masterly wet shave
      that ended in a splash of rose water
      and a customary head massage
      and left me ready to face the crowds.

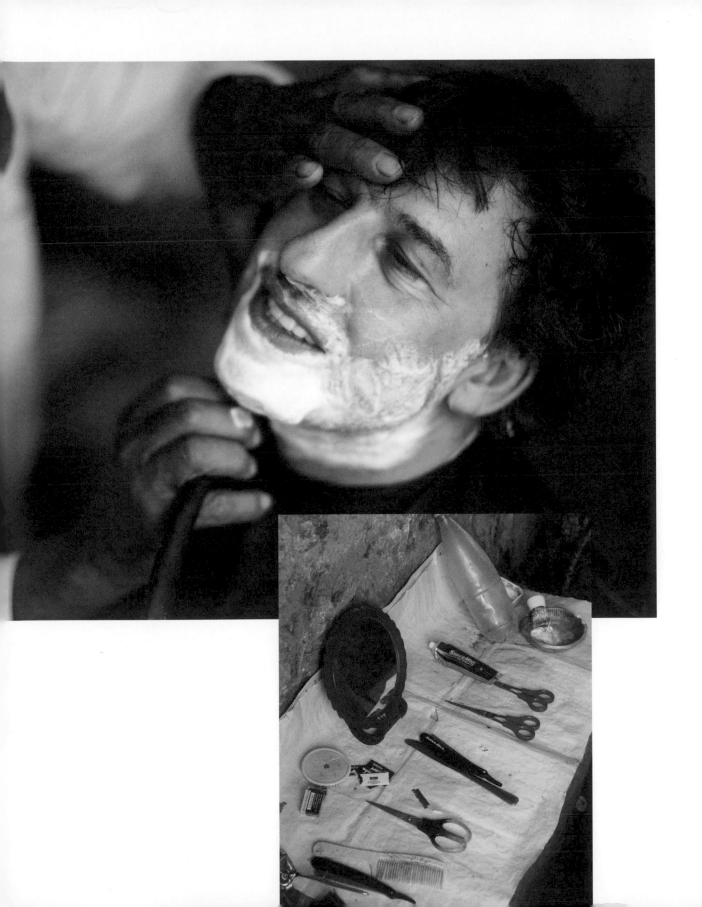

Serves 4
- 4 sheets warkha pastry
  or 8 sheets filo pastry
- olive oil, for frying

Filling
- 200g (7oz/approx 1 cup) soft
  goat's cheese
- zest and juice of 1 orange
- 2 tablespoons unblanched
  almonds, finely chopped
- ½ tablespoon rosemary,
  finely chopped
- 2 tablespoons clear
  runny honey

Sauce
- juice of 1 orange
- 1 tablespoon clear
  runny honey

To serve
- ground cinnamon
- orange zest

Goat's Cheese & Honey Brik

To make the filling, combine the goat's cheese, orange juice and zest, almonds, rosemary and honey in a bowl and mix well.

Take a sheet of warkha and fold the sides in about 4cm (1½in) to make a 24cm (9½in) square. Place a quarter of the filling in the centre of a pastry square, then fold the pastry over to form a triangle. Repeat this process with your remaining ingredients to make four more triangular briks.

If using filo pastry, which tends to be a large rectangular shape, cut the eight sheets in half. For each brik, take a stack of four cut sheets and fold them in half to form a square. Make the brik as you do when using warkha pastry, but moisten the edges with a little melted butter or olive oil to make them stick together.

Fill a large frying pan with olive oil to one-third of the way up the side of the pan. Place over a medium heat. When hot, carefully drop the briks into the pan and fry for about 5–7 minutes, turning once, until the pastry is golden brown. Depending on the size of your frying pan, you may need to fry the briks in batches. Once all the briks have been fried, transfer them to serving plates.

Discard the olive oil from the frying pan. To make the sauce, deglaze the pan by adding the orange juice and honey, stirring over a high heat until the sauce thickens. Drizzle the sauce over the briks and serve immediately with a dusting of cinnamon and a sprinkling of orange zest.

Tuna & Egg Brik

To make the filling, add the olive oil to a pan and fry the onion over a medium heat until softened. Add the remaining ingredients, season generously with salt and pepper, and cook, stirring occasionally, for a further 5 minutes.

To make the dip, mix the harissa and yoghurt in a serving bowl. Set aside until ready to use.

Take a sheet of warkha and fold the sides in about 4cm (1½in) to make a 24cm (9½in) square. Place a quarter of the filling in the middle of the pastry, making a slight well to hold the egg so that it does not run out over the filling. Place an egg in the well and fold over the pastry to form a triangle shape.

If using filo pastry, which tends to be a large rectangular shape, cut the eight sheets in half. For each brik, take a stack of four cut sheets and fold them in half to form a square. Make the briks as you do when using warkha pastry, but moisten the edges with a little melted butter or olive oil to make them stick together.

Fill a large frying pan to one-third of the way up the sides with olive oil. Then heat the oil over a medium heat. When hot, carefully drop the briks into the pan and fry for about 5–7 minutes, turning once, until the pastry is golden brown and the egg is just cooked. Depending on the size of your frying pan, you may need to fry the briks in batches. Once all the briks have been fried, transfer to serving plates.

Serve immediately with the Harissa & Yoghurt Dip on the side and a wedge of lemon.

Serves 4
- 4 sheets warkha pastry or 8 sheets filo pastry
- 4 eggs
- olive oil, for frying

Filling
- 2 tablespoons extra-virgin olive oil
- 1 medium sized onion, finely chopped
- 250g (9oz/approx 1 cup) tinned tuna, drained
- 1 tablespoon tomato purée
- 1 teaspoon ground cumin
- 1 teaspoon ground ginger
- 1 tablespoon capers, drained
- ½ tablespoon harissa (see page 267)
- 1 tablespoon flat-leaf parsley, finely chopped
- 1 tablespoon fresh coriander (cilantro), finely chopped
- sea salt
- freshly ground black pepper

Harissa & Yoghurt Dip
- 1 tablespoon harissa (see page 267)
- 6 tablespoons thick Greek-style yoghurt

To serve
- a wedge of lemon

Find the recipe for Harissa on page 267.

Asparagus Frittata

Serves 2

Preheat the oven to 180°C (350°F). Whisk **6 eggs** with a little **sea salt** and **freshly ground black pepper** and set aside. Heat **1 tablespoon extra-virgin olive oil** and **1 tablespoon butter** in a 19cm (7½in) ovenproof frying pan or cast iron dish over medium heat, then sauté **1 small bunch asparagus, trimmed**, for 5 minutes. Add the prepared eggs, cook for 3 minutes and then bake in the preheated oven for 15–20 minutes until golden and fluffy. Serve hot or cold with **a drizzle of harissa** (see page 267).

Courgette Frittata

Serves 2

Preheat the oven to 180°C (350°F). Whisk **6 eggs** with a little **sea salt** and **freshly ground black pepper** and set aside. Heat **1 tablespoon extra-virgin olive oil** and **1 tablespoon butter** in a 19cm (7½in) ovenproof frying pan or cast iron dish over medium heat, then sauté **2 small courgettes (zucchinis), thinly sliced**, for 2–3 minutes. Add the prepared eggs, cook for 3 minutes and then bake in the preheated oven for 15–20 minutes until golden and fluffy. Serve hot or cold with **a drizzle of harissa** (see page 267).

Salads
& Vegetables

Every sit-down meal in Morocco starts with
a satisfying and dazzling array of small dishes
of colourful salads. Vegetables are prepared in
every which way – raw and grated, boiled and
mashed, chopped and mixed, stuffed and baked,
grilled or roasted then dressed simply with
pungent olive oil, fresh lemon juice or vinegar,
some chopped herbs and a little seasoning.
They're a brilliantly healthy and addictive
way to start any meal.

Orange & Fennel Salad

Serves 4

Peel and segment **3 oranges**, then trim and thinly slice **1 fennel bulb**. Combine the slices from both in a bowl, then dress with **5 tablespoons extra-virgin olive oil** and the **juice of 1 orange**. Season generously with **sea salt** and **freshly ground black pepper** and mix well before serving.

Grated Carrot & Orange Salad

Serves 4

Peel **4 large carrots**, then grate and transfer to a bowl. Add the juice of **3 oranges**, **2 teaspoons ground cumin** and **4 tablespoons extra-virgin olive oil**. Toss to combine and season generously with **sea salt** and **freshly ground black pepper**, transfer to a serving bowl and sprinkle with **shredded mint leaves**.

Radish & Orange Salad

Serves 4

Peel and segment **3 oranges**, then trim and thinly slice a **bunch of radishes** and **1 red onion**. Mix the oranges, radishes and onions in a bowl, then add **5 tablespoons extra-virgin olive oil**. Season generously with **sea salt**, then mix well and serve.

Cauliflower & Olive Salad

Serves 4

Boil **600g (1lb 5oz) cauliflower florets** in salted water until tender. Drain and transfer to a bowl with **100g (3½oz/ ⅔ cup) mixed olives**. Add **1 teaspoon ground coriander (cilantro)**, **1 teaspoon ground turmeric** and **½ teaspoon ground ginger**, and season with **sea salt** and **freshly ground black pepper**.

Drizzle with **4 tablespoons extra-virgin olive oil** and the **juice of ½ a lemon**, then toss to combine and serve.

Cauliflower Croquettes

Serves 4–6 (makes 16 Croquettes)

Remove the crusts from **1 slice of white bread** and soak in a little water. Trim **1kg (2lb) cauliflower**, roughly chop and boil in salted water until soft. Transfer to a large bowl and break it up with your fingers until quite fine, but with a little texture.

Mix in the soaked bread, **100g breadcrumbs (3½oz/2 cups)**, **3 tablespoons chopped flat-leaf parsley**, **½ teaspoon paprika** and **½ teaspoon ground cumin**. Season generously with **sea salt** and **freshly ground black pepper**. Add a generous **slug of extra-virgin olive oil** and **2 beaten eggs**, and stir to combine thoroughly.

Put **200g breadcrumbs (7oz/4 cups)**, **100g (3½oz/approx ⅔ cup) plain (all-purpose) flour** and **1 beaten egg** in three separate bowls. Take a small handful of the cauliflower mixture (about a tablespoon), press into a small ball and flatten slightly. Toss gently in the flour, then dip into the egg and finally roll in the breadcrumbs. Repeat until all the cauliflower mixture is used. Place on a tray and refrigerate for 1 hour.

Place a heavy-bottomed saucepan over medium heat and pour in enough oil so that it's about an inch deep. When the oil is hot, gently lower the croquettes into the pan (you will probably have to do a couple of batches). Once the croquettes are golden on the bottom, turn over and cook the other side. Remove from the pan when they are golden on both sides, take out the pan and place on a piece of kitchen towel to absorb the excess oil.

Stir **2 teaspoons harissa** (see page 267) through **250g (9oz/1 cup) thick Greek-style yoghurt** and serve with the hot croquettes.

Cauliflower Salad

Serves 4

Boil **600g (1lb 5oz) cauliflower florets** in salted water until tender. Drain and transfer to a bowl with **½ tablespoon finely chopped flat-leaf parsley** and **1 teaspoon each of ground turmeric** and **ground coriander (cilantro)**. Season with **sea salt** and **freshly ground black pepper**. Drizzle with **4 tablespoons extra-virgin olive oil** and the **juice of ½ a lemon**, and combine well before serving.

Avocado, Persimmon & Melon Salad

Serves 4

This is not a typical Moroccan salad but I saw some inventive female cooks prepare it one day at the *riad* (traditional Moroccan house) where we stayed.

Stone, peel and slice **1 ripe avocado**, **1 ripe persimmon** and **1 ripe mango**. Place them in a bowl with **2 tablespoons extra-virgin olive oil** and the **juice of ½ lemon**. Season generously with **sea salt** and **freshly ground black pepper**, sprinkle with **finely chopped flat-leaf parsley** and serve.

Cabbage, Walnut & Sultana Salad

Serves 4

Roughly chop **400g (14oz) cabbage** and **100g (3½oz/ approx 1 cup) walnuts** and stir in a bowl with **2 tablespoons sultanas**. Add **4 tablespoons extra-virgin olive oil** and **2 tablespoons cider vinegar**, season with **sea salt** and **freshly ground black pepper**, mix well and serve.

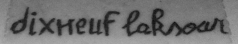

Green Bean Salad

Serves 4

Using a bean cutter, slice **450g (1lb) green beans.** (If you
don't have one, slice them lengthways as thinly as you can).
Boil the beans in salted water until just tender, then drain and
transfer to a bowl with **1 roughly chopped red onion.**
Season with **sea salt** and **freshly ground black pepper,**
then drizzle with **4 tablespoons extra-virgin olive oil**
and the **juice of ½ lemon.**

Before serving, top with **1 tablespoon roughly chopped
coriander (cilantro),** including flowery tips if available.

Broad Bean Salad

Serves 4

Crush **1 teaspoon dried mint** using a mortar and pestle.
Drain **800g (1lb 12oz) tinned broad beans** (or fresh when
available) and add to a bowl with the dried mint,
**1 tablespoon finely chopped fresh mint, 1 tablespoon
argan oil, 2 tablespoons extra-virgin olive oil** and the
juice of ½ lemon. Toss to combine, season generously with
sea salt and **freshly ground black pepper** and transfer to
a serving bowl.

Haricot Bean & Harissa Salad

Serves 4

Drain **800g (1lb 12oz) tinned haricot beans** and transfer to
a bowl with **1 tablespoon harissa** (see page 267) and mix
well to combine. Add **100ml (3½fl oz/approx ½ cup)
extra-virgin olive oil** and the **juice of 1 lemon,** and season
with **sea salt** and **freshly ground black pepper** to taste.
Combine well before serving.

Grated Beetroot & Carrot Salad

Serves 4

Peel and grate **1 large carrot** and **1 large beetroot (beets)**. Combine in a bowl with **1 teaspoon ground ginger**, **2 tablespoons pomegranate juice**, **2 tablespoons cider vinegar** and **4 tablespoons extra-virgin olive oil**. Season generously with **sea salt** and **freshly ground black pepper** and transfer to a serving bowl.

Beetroot & Purslane Salad

Serves 4

The leaf vegetable purslane can be found in specialist Middle Eastern stores or found wild. Boil **450g (1lb) beetroot (beets)** in salted water until tender, then drain, peel and chop. Combine in a bowl with **80g (3oz) purslane** and season with **sea salt** and **freshly ground black pepper**. Dress with **5 tablespoons extra-virgin olive oil** and **2 tablespoons white wine vinegar** before serving.

Glazed Carrot Salad

Serves 4

Peel **600g (1lb 5oz) carrots** and cut into long batons. Cook them in boiling salted water until tender then drain in a colander. Heat **4 tablespoons extra-virgin olive oil** and **2 tablespoons granulated sugar** in a large frying pan over medium heat for a few minutes, then add the carrots, **¼ teaspoon ground ginger** and **1 tablespoon finely chopped coriander (cilantro)**. Cook, carefully stirring for 5 minutes. Transfer to a plate, serve hot or cold.

Pomegranate & Red Onion Salad

Serves 4–6
Cut **2 ripe pomegranates** in quarters, then use the back of a spoon to knock the seeds out into a bowl. Peel and thinly slice **450g (1lb) red onions**, then add to the pomegranate. Toss to combine, season generously with **sea salt** and **freshly ground black pepper** and transfer to a serving bowl. Marinate for about 20 minutes before serving.

Courgette Salad

Serves 4
Boil **500g (approx 1lb) pale green Lebanese courgettes (zucchinis)** in plenty of boiling salted water until tender, for about 15 minutes. Drain in a colander and allow to cool before cutting into thin slices lengthways with a sharp knife. Transfer to a bowl, add **3 finely chopped garlic cloves**, **1 teaspoon ground cumin, 6 tablespoons extra-virgin olive oil** and the **juice of 1 lemon**. Season generously with **sea salt** and **freshly ground black pepper**, mix well and serve.

Grated Cucumber Salad

Serves 4
Combine **¼ teaspoon ground cumin** and **1 teaspoon sea salt** in a small bowl. Peel and grate **1 small cucumber**, then add to a bowl with **3 tablespoons extra-virgin olive oil** and the **juice of ½ lemon** and mix well. Add **1 thinly sliced red onion**, sprinkle with the **cumin salt** and serve.

Swiss Chard & Black Olive Salad

Serves 4

Using a knife, separate the stems and the leaves from **800g (1lb 12oz) Swiss chard**, then roughly chop both, keeping them separate. Bring a saucepan of salted water to the boil.

Meanwhile, using the coarse side of a box grater, grate **1 tomato** into a bowl, discarding the skin.

Add the Swiss chard stems to the boiling water and cook for 5 minutes before adding the leaves. Cook until tender, about 10–12 minutes, then drain and transfer to a bowl.

Heat **3 tablespoons extra-virgin olive oil** in a frying pan over a medium heat. Add the grated tomato and cook for 2 minutes before adding all the Swiss chard and cooking for a further 2 minutes, stirring well. Transfer to a serving bowl, add **100g (3½oz/⅔ cup) black olives**, **1 tablespoon harissa** (see page 267), **sea salt** and **freshly ground black pepper** to taste. Combine mixture well before serving hot or cold.

Potato & Olive Salad

Serves 4

Peel **450g (1lb) potatoes**, then roughly chop and boil in salted water until tender. Drain and transfer to a bowl, adding **200g (7oz/1⅓ cups) olives**, **4 tablespoons extra-virgin olive oil** and **2 tablespoons red wine vinegar**. Season with **sea salt** and **freshly ground black pepper**, toss to combine and transfer to a serving bowl.

My favourite enclosed market is in the Mellah (Marrakesh's old Jewish quarter) where you can find inspiration for seasonal recipes. The vegetable stalls are the place to start; huge bunches of artichokes or cardoons can be added to beef or lamb tagines; radishes, carrots and beetroot for simple grated raw salads; purslane, dandelion and mallow for unusual combinations with herbs and preserved lemons; and juicy pomegranates and oranges for sorbets and jellies.

hand-painted shop signs

Cardoons   smiling stall holders

preserved lemons   Artichokes

bunches of radishes

Chickens ready for plucking

Wizened black olives

Violet olives

pigeons for bistilla

the sharpest butchers knives

the warkha pastry boys

Chilli pickles

At 'La Perle D'Olives' the smiling stallholder offers all sorts of jars of different preserved lemons, pickles and olives. A few stalls down, they make fresh warkha pastry for bistillas and briouats just before you enter the hall where they sell fresh chickens, pigeons and ducks for those who want the experience of choosing a live bird to cook. There's also some surprisingly fresh seafood on offer.

Baby Spinach, Preserved Lemon & Olive Salad

Serves 4

Boil **500g (approx 1lb 2oz) baby spinach leaves** in salted water until tender, then drain. Transfer to a bowl, then add **100g (3½ oz/⅔ cup) mixed olives**, and the **chopped peel from ½ preserved lemon** (see page 253). Dress the salad with **3 tablespoons extra-virgin olive oil** and the **juice of ½ lemon**. Season to taste with **sea salt** and **freshly ground black pepper** and serve.

Mallow, Preserved Lemon & Olive Salad

Serves 4

Mallow is used in soups and salads throughout the Middle East and North Africa, especially in Egypt where it's known as *melokhia*. It can be found wild, is easily grown and available fresh or frozen from specialist Middle Eastern shops.

Boil **500g (approx 1lb) fresh mallow** in salted water until tender, then drain and roughly chop. Transfer to a bowl then add **100g (3½oz/⅔ cup) mixed olives**, and the **chopped peel from ½ preserved lemon** (see page 253). Dress the salad with **2 tablespoons extra-virgin olive oil**, **1 tablespoon argan oil** and the **juice of ½ lemon**. Season to taste with **sea salt** and **freshly ground black pepper** and serve.

Herb Salad with Preserved Lemon Dressing

Serves 2

First make a dressing by combining **1 roughly chopped preserved lemon** (see page 253), **1 tablespoon za'atar spice mix** (available from specialist delis and stores), **yoghurt dressing**, **4 tablespoons extra-virgin olive oil** and **2 tablespoons cider vinegar** in a bowl. Place **80g (3oz) lamb's lettuce** (*mâche*) in a serving bowl with **80g (3oz) mixed baby herbs** (basil, amaranth and coriander/cilantro all work well). Just before serving, pour over the dressing and toss quickly.

Tomato, Egg & Anchovy Salad

Serves 4

Peel and finely slice **1 red onion**, then combine in a bowl with **4 large chopped tomatoes**, a small handful of **black olives**, **2 quartered hard-boiled eggs** and **8 boquerones** (Spanish-style marinated anchovies). Season generously with **sea salt**, **freshly ground black pepper** and **1 teaspoon ground cumin**. Dress with **4 tablespoons extra-virgin olive oil** and the **juice of 1 lemon**. Mix tomatoes, onion, olives, eggs and anchovies together in a bowl. Carefully toss to combine before serving.

Caramelised Tomatoes

Serves 4

Plunge **1kg (2lb 3oz) tomatoes** into a saucepan of boiling water until the skins begin to blister, just a few minutes, then use a slotted spoon to transfer them to a bowl of iced water. Carefully drain in a colander and remove the skins. Halve the tomatoes and remove the seeds. Heat **2 tablespoons extra-virgin olive oil** in a large frying pan with **1 teaspoon ground cinnamon** and **2 tablespoons granulated sugar** and cook for 3 minutes. Add the tomato halves, then cook for 20–30 minutes over a low heat, stirring occasionally, until mixture reduces and caramelises. Transfer to a serving dish and allow to cool before sprinkling with **toasted sesame seeds**.

Chopped Tomato & Cucumber Salad

Serves 2

Deseed and finely chop **1 large tomato**, then finely slice **1 small red onion** and **1 Lebanese cucumber**. Add to a bowl with **2 tablespoons finely chopped flat-leaf parsley**, **4 tablespoons extra-virgin olive oil** and the **juice of 1 lemon**. Season generously with **sea salt** and **freshly ground black pepper** and toss before serving.

Lentil, Lemon & Chilli Salad

Serves 4

Cook **380g (13oz/approx 2 cups) lentils** in boiling salted water until tender. Drain and transfer to a bowl with the **segments from 1 lemon** and **1 deseeded, sliced green chilli**. Add the **juice of ½ lemon, 6 tablespoons extra-virgin olive oil** and then season with **sea salt** and **freshly ground black pepper**. Mix well before serving.

Lemon, Onion & Parsley Salad

Serves 4

Peel and segment **4 lemons**, then place in another bowl with **1 thinly sliced red onion** and **6 tablespoons finely chopped flat-leaf parsley**. Season with **cumin salt** (page 261) and transfer to a serving bowl.

See more Moroccan grains and pulses on page 291.

Lemon, Date & Olive Salad

Serves 4

Peel and segment **3 lemons**, then add to a bowl with **100g (3½ oz/ ⅔ cup) roughly chopped pitted dates, 100g (3½ oz/ ⅔ cup) green olives, 5 tablespoons extra-virgin olive oil** and the **juice of 1 lemon**. Season generously with **sea salt** and **freshly ground black pepper** and mix well before serving.

The Majorelle Garden,
  designed in the 1920s
by French painter
  Jacques Majorelle,
is notable for the intense
cobalt blue colours
  on its walls and buildings.

  Restored by
  Yves Saint Laurent
    and his partner
Pierre Bergé during
  the 1980s, it's on the
  tourist trail now but still
reduces one for a few hours –
  a shady haven of succulents
and trailing bougainvillea
  away from the heat outside.

Peaceful streams
and fountains
and cooing turtle doves
relax you

Roast Pumpkin Salad

Serves 4

Preheat your oven to 200°C (400°F). Peel and remove the seeds from **500g (approx 1lb) pumpkin**, then thinly slice the flesh. Place **1 teaspoon each dried mint**, **ground cumin** and **ground ginger** in a mortar with **½ teaspoon each dried chilli flakes**, **ground cinnamon** and **cumin seeds** and pound with a pestle for a few minutes. Season with **sea salt** and **freshly ground black pepper**, then add **3 tablespoons extra-virgin olive oil** and mix well. Transfer to a bowl, add the pumpkin slices and rub the mixture over the pumpkin.

Place the pumpkin slices on a roasting tray, drizzle over any remaining spice mixture, then roast for 20 minutes, or until tender.

Transfer pumpkin slices to a plate and allow to cool before drizzling with **a little extra-virgin olive oil**.

Chickpea Dip

Serves 4

Drain **800g (1lb 12oz) tinned chickpeas (garbanzos)** and place in the bowl of a food processor with **1 teaspoon ground cumin** and **3 tablespoons extra-virgin olive oil**. Blend to a rough paste, season with **sea salt** and **freshly ground black pepper** and then transfer to a bowl. Heat another **3 tablespoons olive oil** in a frying pan over medium heat and sauté **1 thinly sliced onion** until softened and beginning to go a golden brown colour, for about 5–7 minutes. Add the onion to the chickpea (garbanzo) mixture, combine well and serve with **cumin salt** (see page 261) sprinkled on top.

Fried Aubergine Salad

Serves 4

Thickly slice **500g (approx 1lb) aubergines (eggplants)** and chop into 2cm (½in) pieces. Heat **6 tablespoons olive oil** in a large frying pan over a medium heat, then add **2 thinly sliced garlic cloves, ½ tablespoon dried oregano** and the aubergine (eggplant). Fry for about 8–10 minutes, turning frequently, until softened and tender. Transfer to a bowl, add the **juice of ½ lemon**, season with **sea salt** and serve.

Zaalouk

Serves 4

Trim then partly peel **750g (1lb 10oz) aubergines (eggplants)**, then cut them into thick slices. Lightly salt the slices and place in a colander to drain for 20 minutes, then rinse well and pat dry with kitchen paper.

Heat **5 tablespoons extra-virgin olive oil** in a large frying pan over medium heat and fry the aubergine (eggplant) slices, in batches if necessary, turning occasionally, or until tender and beginning to go a golden brown colour, for about 8 minutes. Transfer to a large bowl and mash.

With the coarse side of a box grater, grate **700g (1lb 8oz) tomatoes** until you are left with just the skins, and transfer tomato mixture to a bowl. Heat **1½ tablespoons extra-virgin olive oil** in the frying pan over medium heat. Add the tomato mixture with **1 teaspoon each ground cumin** and **paprika** then season generously with **sea salt** and **freshly ground black pepper** and cook for about 15–20 minutes or until sauce thickens.

Transfer the tomatoes to the mashed aubergines (eggplants) and add another **drizzle of olive oil**. Combine the mixture well, season to taste and serve hot or cold with **a good squeeze of lemon**.

Mechouia Grilled Vegetable Salad

Serves 6

Though more common in Tunisia and Algeria, they also grill vegetables on small charcoal braziers in Morocco to obtain the sensual smoky flavours found in this simple salad. Usually, all the grilled vegetables are roughly chopped with plenty of finely chopped garlic and preserved lemon rind, but for a change I keep them whole so they can be used as a side vegetable to cooked meats.

Heat a barbecue grill or cast iron griddle pan to medium. **Halve 4 ripe tomatoes and quarter two more.** Halve and deseed **4 long green peppers (capsicums)**, then halve **3 small red onions** with the skin left on. Grill the tomatoes, peppers and onion, turning frequently, until tender and blackened all over. Transfer to a bowl and add **2 tablespoons capers**.

Make a dressing by combining **2 finely chopped garlic cloves**, **½ teaspoon ras el hanout** (see page 258), **3 tablespoons extra-virgin olive oil** and the **juice of 1 lemon**. Mix well, season with **sea salt** and **freshly ground black pepper**, then stir in the finely chopped rind of **½ preserved lemon** (see page 253). Drizzle the dressing over the grilled vegetables, sprinkle with **finely chopped coriander (cilantro) leaves** (and flowers if you have them) and serve while still warm.

Grilled Pepper Salad

Serves 4

Heat a barbecue grill or cast iron griddle pan to medium. Grill **300g (10½oz) long green peppers (capsicums)**, turning occasionally, until tender, for about 8–10 minutes. Transfer the peppers to a wooden board, remove skins and deseed before chopping. Place in a mortar and pound with a pestle for a few minutes, but don't purée them. Add **1 tablespoon finely sliced flat-leaf parsley, 2 chopped garlic cloves**, and the **juice of ½ lemon**. Season with **sea salt** and mix well before serving.

Moroccan Tuna Niçoise with Roasted Tomatoes

Serves 4
- 8 ripe tomatoes
- 8 garlic cloves, crushed
- 2 tablespoons capers, drained
- ¼ tablespoon ras el hanout (see page 258)
- 2 tablespoons flat-leaf parsley, roughly chopped
- 3 tablespoons extra-virgin olive oil
- sea salt
- freshly ground black pepper
- 250g (9oz/approx 1½ cups) green beans, trimmed and blanched
- 250g (9oz/approx 1 cup) tinned tuna, drained
- 3 boiled eggs, halved, peeled and thinly sliced
- 100g (3½ oz/⅔ cup) handful mixed olives, drained then crushed

Dressing
- 2 small red onions
- juice of 1 lemon
- 6 tablespoons extra virgin olive oil
- 2 tablespoons flat-leaf parsley, finely chopped
- sea salt
- freshly ground black pepper

To serve
- toasted or grilled Arab-style flatbread

Preheat the oven to 180°C (350°F). Cut four of the tomatoes in half and the other four into quarters, and place in a roasting tin. Add the garlic, capers, ras el hanout, parsley, olive oil and season with salt and pepper.

Combine mixture well then roast for 40 minutes, until the tomatoes are cooked. Remove from the oven and allow to cool.

Meanwhile to make the dressing, place the onions in a bowl with the lemon juice. Add the other ingredients and combine. Season with salt and pepper.

To assemble the salad, place the tomatoes on a platter, add the beans, flaked tuna, boiled eggs and olives. Drizzle over the dressing and serve with flatbread.

Stuffed Baby Vegetables

You can use other vegetables such as aubergines, onions, carrots and potatoes in this dish. If you can't find round courgettes, use small courgettes hollowed out with an apple corer.

Slice the very tops off the tomatoes, courgettes and peppers and put them to one side. Carefully scoop out the pulp and seeds from the tomatoes and courgettes with a teaspoon to allow room for stuffing. Next, remove the cores and seeds from the peppers with a small knife.

To make the Spicy Tomato Sauce, use a box grater and coarsely grate the tomatoes into a bowl, discarding skins. Heat the olive oil in a large saucepan over a medium heat and sauté the onion and garlic until softened, for about 5 minutes. Add the grated tomato, tomato purée and harissa and cook, stirring occasionally, for 5 minutes. Season generously with salt and pepper. Add the water, lower the heat and simmer for 20 minutes, or until sauce reduces and thickens. Transfer to a jug and allow to cool.

For the stuffing, combine all the ingredients in a bowl and season generously with salt and pepper and mix well.

Fill the tomatoes, courgettes and peppers with stuffing, replace tops and carefully place in a large saucepan. Pour the tomato sauce around the vegetables, cover the saucepan with a lid and cook over a medium heat for 30 minutes or until vegetables are tender and the stuffing is cooked. Allow to cool before serving.

Serves 6
- 8 small tomatoes
- 9 small round courgettes (zucchinis)
- 8 small green peppers (capsicums)

Spicy Tomato Sauce
- 3 large tomatoes
- 3 tablespoons extra-virgin olive oil
- 1 large red onion, peeled and finely chopped
- 4 garlic cloves, peeled and finely chopped
- 1 tablespoon tomato purée
- ½ tablespoon harissa (see page 267)
- sea salt
- freshly ground black pepper
- 250ml (1 cup) water

Stuffing
- 800g (1lb 12oz) minced lamb or beef
- 170g (6oz/approx 1½ cups) long-grain rice, cooked
- 1 large onion, peeled and finely chopped
- 5 garlic cloves, peeled and finely chopped
- 5 tablespoons flat-leaf parsley, finely chopped
- 1 tablespoon ground cumin
- 1 tablespoon ground ginger
- 2 teaspoons paprika
- 3 tablespoons extra-virgin olive oil
- sea salt
- freshly ground black pepper

Street Food & Snacks

Anyone travelling to Morocco will see people everywhere eating in the street. There is always a plethora of food establishments, often clustered around the chaotic markets – from tiny hole-in-the-wall grill joints cooking skewers of meat, to fried fish and vegetable stalls, and makeshift stands with rows of bubbling tagines over charcoal braziers. This is where you will truly experience some of the famed Moroccan hospitality as you make friends over some of the country's most delicious food.

Serves 4 (makes 12 Croquettes)

- 1kg (2lb 3oz) potatoes, peeled and boiled
- ½ teaspoon paprika
- ½ teaspoon ground cumin
- ½ teaspoon ground turmeric
- flour, for dusting
- 2 hard-boiled eggs, peeled and cut into eighths
- 150g (5oz/approx 2 cups) fine breadcrumbs
- 1 egg
- vegetable oil, for frying

Filling
- 2 tablespoons olive oil
- 200g (7oz) minced (ground) beef
- 2 garlic cloves, finely chopped
- 1 small onion, finely chopped
- ½ teaspoon ground cinnamon
- ¼ teaspoon ground nutmeg
- 1 tablespoon flat-leaf parsley, finely chopped
- 1 teaspoon tomato purée
- 150ml (5fl oz/⅔ cup) cold water
- sea salt
- freshly ground black pepper
- 40g (1½oz/approx ½ cup) fine breadcrumbs
- 1 egg, beaten

To serve
- lemon wedges

Stuffed Potato Croquettes

You can also add chopped green olives to the filling and serve with harissa dipping sauce (see page 267) if you want.

To make the filling, heat the oil in a frying pan over a medium heat, then add the minced beef and brown for 5 minutes. Transfer to a bowl.

Add the garlic and onion to the frying pan and sauté for about 3–5 minutes, or until softened. Add the cinnamon, nutmeg, parsley, tomato purée, cooked minced beef and 150ml water and season with salt and pepper. Cook for about 10 minutes until the liquid reduces to a thick consistency, then transfer to a bowl and set aside to cool. Once cool, add breadcrumbs and egg and mix until combined.

Mash the potatoes. Add the paprika, cumin and turmeric and mix until well combined, then knead into a dough.

Roll the dough out on a lightly floured surface until about 1cm (½in) thick, then use a 6cm (2½in) biscuit cutter to make twelve rounds in the dough. Place a heaped teaspoon of the filling in the middle of each round and top with a piece of hard-boiled egg. Fold the potato dough carefully over the filling to create golf ball-like shapes. Repeat the process with the remaining dough and filling. Refrigerate for at least 30 minutes.

Meanwhile, place the breadcrumbs on a plate and beat the egg in a bowl. Remove the croquettes from the refrigerator. Dip each croquette in the beaten egg and then roll in breadcrumbs.

Heat the vegetable oil in a saucepan to 175°C (345°F), then deep-fry the croquettes for about 5 minutes, or until golden coloured. Transfer to kitchen paper to drain, then serve on a platter with lemon wedges.

Serves 4

- 4 Arab-style flatbreads
- extra-virgin olive oil, for smearing and drizzling
- 4 potatoes, peeled whole, boiled then roughly chopped
- 4 eggs, boiled but still soft, peeled and roughly chopped
- 1 teaspoon ground cumin
- sea salt

Egg & Potato Rolls

This is one of my favourite snacks from the Djemaa el Fna square. There are two stalls serving this cheap and cheerful meal to hungry Moroccans. After a hard day's work, you can choose soft- or hard-boiled free-range organic eggs, which are then peeled and combined with just-boiled hot potatoes in a roll and topped with fruity olive oil and cumin salt. It's one of the dishes you won't forget after eating it on the square.

Split open the flatbreads with a sharp knife, then smear olive oil on the inside of each. Add a potato and an egg to each roll, sprinkle with cumin and salt and drizzle with extra olive oil. Press the tops of the flatbreads down and serve.

Spicy Grilled Vegetable Rolls with Chickpea Salad

Serves 4
- 1 tablespoon clear runny honey, warmed
- 1 tablespoon harissa (see page 267)
- 4 baby aubergines (eggplants), sliced lengthways
- 2 green peppers (capsicums), deseeded and sliced
- 2 red peppers (capsicums), deseeded and sliced
- 2 red onions, sliced
- 2 ripe tomatoes, sliced
- 3 courgettes (zucchinis), thinly sliced
- 2 tablespoons extra-virgin olive oil, plus extra for basting
- 2 pieces Arab-style flatbread

Chickpea Salad
- 400g (14oz) tinned chickpeas (garbanzos), drained
- ½ tablespoon paprika
- 1 onion, thinly sliced
- 2 tablespoons flat-leaf parsley, finely chopped
- ½ tablespoon ground cumin
- 5 tablespoons extra-virgin olive oil
- juice of 1 lemon
- sea salt
- freshly ground black pepper

To serve
- salad leaves

To make the chickpea salad, put the chickpeas in a bowl and roughly mash with a fork. Add the remaining ingredients, season with salt and pepper and set aside.

Combine the honey and harissa in a small bowl.

Next, griddle all the vegetables on a barbecue or cast iron griddle pan over a medium heat, basting with olive oil and turning occasionally, for about 10 minutes or until tender and cooked. Season with salt and pepper while cooking.

During the last 5 minutes of cooking the vegetables, baste the aubergines with the harissa-honey mix, and cook for about 3 minutes longer than the other vegetables, or until they begin to blacken and soften.

Split open the flatbreads using a sharp knife and lightly toast.

To assemble, place the vegetables and chickpea salad on the toasted flatbread with some salad leaves.

Chicken Kebabs
with Spicy Avocado Dip

Combine the chicken pieces with the ginger, paprika, turmeric, coriander and olive oil in a bowl and season generously with salt and pepper. Cover with cling film and refrigerate for at least 30 minutes.

Mash the avocado flesh in a bowl with a potato masher or a fork. Add the other ingredients and season with salt and pepper.

Remove the marinated chicken pieces from the refrigerator and thread onto eight metal skewers.

Grill on a barbecue or cast iron griddle pan over medium heat, turning occasionally, for 5–7 minutes or until cooked through and tender.

To assemble, smear the warmed flatbread with the Spicy Avocado Dip, then top with some lettuce leaves and the chicken kebabs. Sprinkle each kebab with finely chopped coriander and a squeeze of lemon juice.

Serves 4
- 3 (about 380g/13oz each) chicken breasts, cut into 2cm (1in) cubes
- 2 tablespoons fresh ginger, finely grated
- 1 tablespoon paprika
- ½ tablespoon turmeric
- 1 teaspoon ground coriander (cilantro)
- 3 tablespoons extra-virgin olive oil
- sea salt
- freshly ground black pepper
- 2 Arab-style flatbreads, warmed
- salad leaves
- 8 metal skewers or 8 wooden skewers (soaked in water)

Spicy Avocado Dip
- 2 ripe avocados, halved and deseeded
- 1 teaspoon ground cumin
- 2 garlic cloves, finely chopped
- 1 fresh green or red chilli, deseeded and finely chopped
- 1 tablespoon fresh coriander (cilantro), finely chopped
- 3 tablespoons extra-virgin olive oil
- juice of 1 lemon, plus extra for squeezing
- sea salt
- freshly ground black pepper

To serve
- coriander (cilantro), finely chopped

Merguez Sausage Baguette

At the grill stalls in Djemaa el Fna square, Merguez sausages are served simply with bread and harissa dipping sauce.

Combine the crème fraîche, Dijon mustard, cornichons and lemon juice in a bowl and season generously with salt and pepper.

Grill or barbecue the Merguez sausages on a barbecue or cast iron griddle pan over a medium heat, basting with a little olive oil and turning occasionally, for about 6–7 minutes or until tender and cooked.

To assemble, smear the baguette with the harissa and crème fraîche mixture. Add the Merguez sausages and some baby green salad leaves, and drizzle with a little olive oil. Cut the baguette in half and serve on two plates.

Serves 2
- 4 tablespoons crème fraîche
- 2 tablespoons Dijon mustard
- 2 tablespoons cornichons, chopped
- juice of ½ lemon
- sea salt
- freshly ground black pepper
- 10 small Merguez sausages
- extra-virgin olive oil, for basting and for drizzling
- 1 baguette, sliced lengthways
- 1 tablespoon of harissa (see page 267)
- 1 small handful mixed baby green salad leaves

Find a recipe for harissa on page 267.

Kefta Sandwich with Chopped Tomato & Cucumber Salad

Serves 4-6
- 500g (1lb 2oz) minced (ground) beef
- 1 small red onion, finely grated
- 1 teaspoon ground cumin
- 1 teaspoon paprika
- ½ teaspoon ground coriander (cilantro)
- ½ tablespoon fresh ginger, finely grated
- 4 tablespoons fresh coriander (cilantro), finely chopped
- sea salt
- freshly ground black pepper
- olive oil, for frying (optional)
- 4-6 Arab-style flatbreads, warmed

Chopped Tomato & Cucumber Salad
Serves 2
- 1 large tomato, deseeded and finely chopped
- 1 small red onion, peeled and thinly sliced
- 1 Lebanese cucumber, thinly sliced
- 2 tablespoons flat-leaf parsley, finely chopped
- 4 tablespoons extra-virgin olive oil
- juice of 1 lemon
- sea salt
- freshly ground black pepper

To serve
- thick Greek-style yoghurt
- harissa (see page 267)

Combine the minced beef, onion, cumin, paprika, ground coriander, ginger and fresh coriander in a bowl. Season generously with salt and pepper and mix well.

Refrigerate for a minimum of 30 minutes before shaping into 16 walnut-sized kefta.

For the Chopped Tomato & Cucumber Salad, combine and toss together the tomato, onion, cucumber and parsley in a bowl. Add the oil and lemon juice, season generously with salt and pepper and mix well.

Grill the kefta on a barbecue or a cast iron griddle pan over a medium heat, turning occasionally, for about 5-7 minutes or until cooked. Alternatively, fry in a large frying pan with a little oil over a medium heat.

To assemble, split open the flatbreads with a sharp knife and smear the insides with a little yoghurt and harissa. Divide the kefta and Chopped Tomato & Cucumber Salad onto the breads, then gently push the tops down.

smoky charcoal grills

Crowds of local Marrakchi

freshly squeezed orange juice

fresh mint

Bowls of bean and lentil soups

scented teas

For one of the world's best street food experiences, simply head for the famous Djemaa el Fna Square. It is one of the main attractions of Marrakesh, a 12-hectare trapezoidal-shaped area that's home to acrobats, snake charmers, fortune tellers, faith healers, monkey trainers and the occasional pick-pockets who work the crowds. Still a place where public executions were held in the early 20th century, today it's a hypnotic roller-coaster ride of adventurous eating at its lively food stalls.

Empty snail shells everywhere

the glittering Koutoubia Mosque

fish and chips

Magicians enthralling the crowds

children lost and found again

In the shadow of the Koutoubia Mosque, locals stop at favourite stalls to eat steaming bowls of snails scented with cinnamon and cumin, offal every which way, freshly fried fish and chips, mixed grills of lamb and beef kefta, Merguez sausages and chicken kebabs all washed down with steaming glasses of mint tea.

Fish Kefta

Serves 4 (makes 8 Kefta)

- 1 slice white bread, crusts removed
- 500g (1lb 2oz) cod or other firm fish fillets
- 1½ teaspoons ground cumin
- 1 teaspoon turmeric
- 2 garlic cloves, crushed
- 1 egg, beaten
- 40g (1½oz/approx ½ cup) fine breadcrumbs
- zest from 1 lemon
- 1 tablespoon flat-leaf parsley, finely chopped
- 1 tablespoon fresh coriander (cilantro), finely chopped
- sea salt
- freshly ground black pepper
- 3 tablespoons plain (all-purpose) flour, for dusting
- extra-virgin olive oil, for frying

To serve
- lemon wedges, to garnish

You could also serve these in rolls with salad and harissa mayo.

Soak the slice of bread in a small bowl of water for 5 minutes, then remove and squeeze out all the liquid and transfer to a large bowl.

Add the cod, cumin, turmeric, garlic, egg, breadcrumbs, lemon zest, parsley and coriander to the bread. Season generously with salt and pepper and combine well. Cover with cling film and refrigerate for at least 30 minutes, then mould the mixture into eight 5cm (2in) balls.

Place the plain flour onto a plate, then roll the kefta in the flour to coat.

Heat some olive oil in a large frying pan over medium heat, add the kefta and fry for about 8–10 minutes, turning occasionally, until golden brown and cooked through.

Transfer to a platter lined with kitchen paper then divide between four plates and serve with a wedge of lemon.

Serves 4
- 60g (2oz/approx ⅓ cup) plain (all-purpose) flour
- 1 generous tablespoon saffron threads, crushed in a mortar and pestle
- 1 tablespoon paprika
- 1 tablespoon turmeric
- ½ tablespoon cayenne pepper
- sea salt
- 600g (1lb 5oz) cod or other firm-fleshed fish fillets, skin on, cut into large chunks or slices
- 5 tablespoons olive oil
- 1 large aubergine (eggplant), sliced

To serve
- lemon wedges

Fried Fish & Aubergines

This classic way of frying fish can be sampled all over Morocco, usually served with fried aubergines and French fries.

Combine the flour, saffron, paprika, turmeric, cayenne pepper and a generous pinch of salt in a large bowl. Coat the fish with the flour mixture and set aside.

Meanwhile, heat the olive oil in a large frying pan over a medium heat and fry the aubergine slices, turning occasionally, for about 8 minutes, or until tender and beginning to turn golden brown. Transfer to kitchen paper and keep warm until ready to serve. Depending on the size of your pan, you may need to cook the aubergine in batches.

Put the cod pieces in the frying pan, adding a little more olive oil if necessary, and cook, turning occasionally, for 8 minutes or until tender. Transfer to kitchen paper.

Place the aubergine and fish on a platter, sprinkle with a little salt and serve with lemon.

Mackerel with Potato, Olive & Preserved Lemon Salad

To make the lemon chermoula, place the garlic, cumin, paprika, saffron, chilli, cayenne pepper, parsley and coriander in a food processor. Season with salt and pepper and blend until well combined. Add the olive oil and lemon juice and blend to a paste. Transfer the mixture to a large bowl.

Add the mackerel to the chermoula and combine. Cover with cling film and refrigerate for at least 30 minutes.

Meanwhile, make the Potato, Olive & Preserved Lemon Salad by combining all the ingredients in a bowl. Season generously with salt and pepper.

Remove the marinated mackerel from the refrigerator. Heat the olive oil in a large frying pan over medium heat, add the marinated mackerel fillets, in batches if necessary. Cook for 6–7 minutes turning the fillets once.

Transfer to a platter, or individual plates, and serve with the Potato, Olive & Preserved Lemon Salad.

Serves 4
- 500g (1lb) mackerel fillets
- 2 tablespoons olive oil, for frying

Lemon Chermoula
- 3 garlic cloves, finely chopped
- 1 teaspoon ground cumin
- ½ teaspoon paprika
- 1 teaspoon saffron threads
- 1 red chilli, deseeded and thinly sliced
- ½ teaspoon cayenne pepper
- 2 tablespoons flat-leaf parsley, finely chopped
- 2 tablespoons fresh coriander (cilantro), finely chopped
- sea salt
- freshly ground black pepper
- 4 tablespoons extra-virgin olive oil
- juice of 1 lemon

Potato, Olive & Preserved Lemon Salad
- 750g (1lb 10oz) potatoes, peeled, diced and boiled
- 150g (5oz/1 cup) olives
- 2 tablespoons capers, drained
- ½ small preserved lemon, thinly sliced (see page 253)
- 4 tablespoons extra-virgin olive oil
- 2 tablespoons red wine vinegar
- sea salt
- freshly ground black pepper

Marinated Sardines

Serves 4

Place **12 (about 1kg/2lb 3oz) sardines**, cleaned and filleted, in a bowl, then add **100ml (3½fl oz/approx ½ cup) extra-virgin olive oil**, **the juice and zest of 1 lemon**, and **1 garlic clove**, thinly sliced. Cover with cling film and marinate in the refrigerator for at least 30 minutes.

Meanwhile, grate **1 ripe tomato** into a bowl using a coarse grater. Discard the tomato skin.

Remove the marinated sardines from the refrigerator and transfer to a serving platter. Sprinkle over **½ teaspoon aniseed or fennel seeds** and season generously with **sea salt** and **freshly ground black pepper**. Add the grated tomato, combine well with the sardines and serve.

*See how to make your own
Preserved lemons on page 253.*

Sardines on Toast with Cherry Tomato & Preserved Lemon Salad

Serves 2

Place **24 cherry tomatoes**, halved, the **rind of ½ preserved lemon** (see page 253) cut into strips, **1 tablespoon capers**, drained, **4 tablespoons extra-virgin olive oil** and the **juice of ½ lemon** in a bowl. Season generously with **sea salt** and **freshly ground black pepper** and mix until well combined.

To assemble, split open **1 Arab-style flatbread**, using a sharp knife, and lightly toast. Divide **125g (4oz) tinned sardines**, drained, between the two halves of flatbread, then top each with the Tomato & Preserved Lemon Salad and serve.

Spicy Squid with Harissa Yoghurt Dip

Serves 4

Combine **400g (14oz) squid**, cleaned and chopped, **2 garlic cloves**, thinly sliced, **4 tablespoons extra-virgin olive oil**, **1 tablespoon fresh coriander (cilantro)**, finely chopped, **1 tablespoon flat-leaf parsley**, finely chopped, **½ tablespoon harissa** (see page 267), **½ teaspoon ground ginger** and **½ teaspoon ground cumin** in a large bowl. Cover with cling film and marinate in the refrigerator for 30 minutes.

Meanwhile, mix **1 tablespoon harissa** and **6 tablespoons thick Greek-style yoghurt** together in a small bowl.

Remove the marinated squid from the refrigerator. Heat some **olive oil** in a large frying pan over a medium heat, then add the marinated squid and cook for 5–7 minutes, or until just tender. Transfer to a serving plate, drizzle any remaining pan juices over the squid and serve with the Harissa Yoghurt Dip.

Spicy Garlic-Lemon Prawns

Serves 4

Combine **6 tablespoons extra-virgin olive oil**, **juice of 1 lemon**, **6 garlic cloves**, chopped, and **1 teaspoon paprika** in a bowl. Add **12 large prawns (shrimp)**, heads removed but shells left on, and mix well. Cover with cling film and marinate in the refrigerator for 1–2 hours.

Meanwhile, get four metal skewers or four wooden skewers (soaked in water to stop them from burning during cooking). Remove the marinated prawns from the refrigerator and thread three prawns onto each skewer. Reserve the marinade. Grill the prawns or cook in a cast iron griddle pan over a medium heat, turning once, for about 6–7 minutes or until cooked.

Transfer the prawns to a platter and drizzle with the remaining marinade. Serve with **rocket (arugula) salad** and **Arab-style flatbread**.

For a truly medieval experience,
visit the tanneries around Fna Fna
in the Debbaghine district.
You're given a bunch of mint
to hold up to your nose
as the smell is overpowering.

There are hundreds of
hole-in-the-ground concrete
vats where skins are soaked,
softened and trampled on
by workers in a mixture
of lime, pigeon dung and
tannin to remove any traces
of flesh and hair.

The skins are then rubbed
with pomegranate and olive oil,
stretched and dried in the sun
then dyed with henna
and other traditional colourants.

It's a harrowing, strangely cathartic
experience and it
makes you think twice
about the leather goods
you buy in the souks.

Moroccan Mixed Grill

Serves 2
- 240g (8oz) chicken breast, cut into 5cm (2in) pieces
- 4 (320g/11oz) lamb chops
- 6 Merguez sausages
- 2 (about 200g/7oz each) sirloin steaks
- 4 tablespoons extra-virgin olive oil, for basting

Lamb Kefta
- 200g (7oz) minced (ground) lamb
- ½ small red onion, finely grated
- ¼ teaspoon ground cumin
- ¼ teaspoon paprika
- ¼ teaspoon ground coriander (cilantro)
- ¼ tablespoon fresh root ginger, finely grated
- 1 tablespoon fresh coriander (cilantro), finely chopped
- sea salt
- freshly ground black pepper
- 4 flat metal skewers or 4 wooden skewers (soaked in water)

To serve
- bread
- harissa (see page 267)

To make the kefta, combine the minced lamb, red onion, cumin, paprika, ground coriander, ginger and fresh coriander in a bowl. Season generously with salt and pepper and mix well. Shape the mince firmly around two flat metal skewers, then refrigerate for at least 30 minutes.

Meanwhile, thread the chicken pieces onto two metal skewers, or two wooden skewers.

Grill or barbecue the lamb kefta, chicken kebabs, lamb chops, Merguez sausages and sirloin steaks over a medium heat on a barbecue or cast iron griddle pan, basting with a little olive oil and turning occasionally, for about 5–10 minutes, or until the meats are tender.

Divide the mixed grill between two plates and serve with bread and harissa.

Harissa with your Moroccan Mixed Grill would be great. See how to make your own on page 267.

Serves 2

- 300g (10½oz) beef fillet,
  cut into 4cm (approx 2in) pieces
- 1 teaspoon harissa (see page 267)
- 1 teaspoon ground cumin
- 1 tablespoon extra-virgin olive oil,
  plus extra for grilling
- sea salt
- freshly ground black pepper
- 8 baby onions, peeled
- 3 tomatoes, halved
- 6 wooden skewers
  (soaked in water)

To serve
- toasted Arab-style flatbread
- lemon wedges

Beef, Onion & Tomato Kebabs

Place the beef pieces in a large bowl with the harissa, cumin and olive oil. Season generously with salt and pepper and mix well. Cover with cling film and marinate in the refrigerator for at least 1 hour.

Remove the marinated beef from the refrigerator and thread onto the skewers.

Place the onions and tomatoes on a barbecue or cast iron griddle pan over a medium heat and cook, basting with a little olive oil and turning occasionally, for about 10–12 minutes, or until tender. Transfer to a plate, cover with aluminium foil and keep warm.

Add the beef skewers to the barbecue or cast iron griddle pan, and cook over a medium heat. Baste the beef skewers with the remaining marinade and turn occasionally, for about 8–10 minutes, or until tender and cooked.

Transfer to two plates and serve with the cooked onion and tomatoes, toasted flatbread and lemon wedges.

Lamb Brochettes with Grated Beetroot & Carrot Salad

Put the cumin, coriander, chilli flakes and olive oil in a large bowl and mix well. Season with salt and pepper, then add the lamb and rub with the marinade ingredients until well coated. Cover with cling film and refrigerate for at least 30 minutes.

Remove the marinated lamb from the refrigerator and thread onto 16 metal skewers, or wooden skewers soaked in water. Place the brochettes on a barbecue or cast iron griddle pan over a medium heat and cook, basting with a little olive oil and turning occasionally, for about 8–10 minutes, or until tender and cooked.

To serve, divide the Grated Beetroot & Carrot Salad onto the plates. Add the Lamb Brochettes and sprinkle with cumin salt.

Find the recipe for Grated Beetroot & Carrot Salad on page 34.

Serves 4
- ½ tablespoon ground cumin
- ½ tablespoon ground coriander (cilantro)
- ½ tablespoon chilli flakes
- 2 tablespoons extra-virgin olive oil
- sea salt
- freshly ground black pepper
- 600g (1lb 5oz) lamb leg or shoulder, trimmed and cut into 5cm (2in) pieces
- 16 metal skewers

To serve
- cumin salt (see page 261)

Serves 2
Chilli Salt
- 1 tablespoon chilli flakes
- ½ tablespoon chilli powder
- ½ teaspoon sea salt

Liver Brochettes
- 2 pieces (about 200g/7oz) caul fat
- 2 (about 400g/14oz) thick slices calves' or lamb's liver
- 2 long red peppers
- extra-virgin olive oil, for basting
- 6 metal skewers or 6 wooden skewers (soaked in water)

Liver Brochettes with Chilli Salt

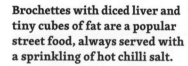

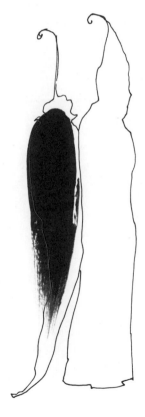

Brochettes with diced liver and tiny cubes of fat are a popular street food, always served with a sprinkling of hot chilli salt.

To make the Chilli Salt, combine the chilli flakes, the chilli powder and salt in a small bowl and set aside until ready to use.

Place the caul fat in a bowl of cold water for 10 minutes. Remove from bowl, dry carefully with kitchen paper and then unfurl onto a wooden board. Place the calves' liver on top and wrap the caul fat around the liver. Cut into strips and thread onto a skewer. Repeat the process with the remaining slice of caul fat and liver and set aside. You should get about six brochettes.

Place the whole red peppers on the barbecue or cast iron griddle pan over a medium heat and cook, basting with a little olive oil and turning occasionally, for about 10–12 minutes, or until tender. Transfer to a plate and cover with aluminium foil to keep warm.

Add the liver brochettes to the barbecue or cast iron grill pan over a medium heat and cook, basting with a little olive oil and turning occasionally, for about 8–10 minutes, or until tender and cooked.

Serve the Liver Brochettes with the grilled peppers and Chilli Salt on the side.

Fried Liver with Onions

For the marinade, place the cumin, coriander and paprika in a mortar. Season generously with salt and pepper, then add the parsley and coriander and pound with a pestle to a rough paste. Add the olive oil and vinegar, combine well and transfer to a bowl. Alternatively, put all the ingredients into a mini food processor and blend into a rough paste.

Add the liver and garlic to the marinade, then mix until the liver is well coated. Cover with cling film and refrigerate for 1 hour.

Meanwhile, heat 2 tablespoons olive oil in a frying pan over a medium heat and sauté the onions for 15–20 minutes or until cooked. Transfer to a bowl, cover with aluminium foil and keep warm.

Heat the remaining oil in the frying pan over medium heat. Add the liver and marinade and cook, turning once, for 5–6 minutes or until cooked.

Transfer the liver to two plates, add the sautéed onions and serve.

Serves 2
- 2 slices (about 400g/14oz) calves' liver, each slice cut into 3 pieces
- 2 garlic cloves, thinly sliced
- 4 tablespoons extra-virgin olive oil, for frying
- 2 large onions, peeled and thinly sliced

Marinade
- ½ teaspoon ground cumin
- ½ teaspoon ground coriander (cilantro)
- ½ teaspoon paprika
- sea salt
- freshly ground black pepper
- ½ tablespoon flat-leaf parsley, roughly chopped
- ½ tablespoon fresh coriander (cilantro), roughly chopped
- 1 tablespoon extra-virgin olive oil
- 2 tablespoons red wine vinegar

Moroccan Steak & Chips with Pickled Cucumbers

Serves 2
- 2 (about 450g/1lb) rib-eye or sirloin steaks
- 500g (approx 1lb 2oz) potatoes, peeled and cut into 1cm (½in) thick pieces and placed in bowl of cold water
- peanut oil, for deep-frying

Marinade
- ½ teaspoon ground cumin
- ½ teaspoon ground coriander (cilantro)
- ½ teaspoon paprika
- 2 garlic cloves, thinly sliced
- 1 tablespoon extra-virgin olive oil, plus extra for frying (optional)
- sea salt
- freshly ground black pepper

Harissa Yoghurt Dip
- 1 tablespoon harissa (see page 267)
- 6 tablespoons thick Greek-style yoghurt

To serve
- Middle Eastern-style long pickled cucumbers, sliced

First, to make the Harissa Yoghurt Dip, mix the harissa and yoghurt in a small bowl and set aside.

For the marinade, put the cumin, coriander, paprika, garlic and olive oil in a large bowl and mix well. Season with salt and pepper, then add the beef steaks and rub with the marinade until well coated. Cover with cling film and refrigerate for 30 minutes.

Remove the marinated beef from the refrigerator and lift the beef out of the marinade. Pan fry the beef in a little olive oil, or grill on a barbecue or cast iron griddle pan over a medium heat for about 5 minutes each side for medium-rare. Add the garlic from the marinade halfway through cooking. Transfer to two serving plates.

Meanwhile, drain the potatoes and pat dry with kitchen paper. Heat the peanut oil in a deep-fryer or large saucepan to 140–150°C (275–300°F). Add the potatoes and cook for 6 minutes, or until cooked through. Transfer to kitchen paper.

Place the chips on the plates with the steaks, and serve with the Harissa Yoghurt Dip and pickled cucumbers.

Beef & Barley Couscous Salad

Use regular couscous or bulghur wheat if you can't find the slightly coarser barley couscous, which is great in salads.

Put the cumin, paprika, coriander, garlic and olive oil in a large bowl and mix well. Season generously with salt and pepper, then add the beef steaks and rub with the marinade until well coated. Cover with cling film and refrigerate for at least 30 minutes.

To make the Barley Couscous Salad, place the barley couscous in a large bowl and pour over boiling water, enough to just cover the couscous. Leave to stand for 30 minutes, or until couscous has absorbed all the water, then fluff up the couscous with a spoon to break up any lumps. Add the chopped lettuce, parsley, coriander, rocket and onion and combine well. Season generously with salt and pepper, then add the olive oil and lemon juice and combine the mixture again.

Remove the marinated beef from the refrigerator and lift the beef out of the marinade. Pan fry the beef in a little olive oil, or grill on a barbecue or cast iron griddle pan over a medium heat for about 5 minutes each side for medium-rare. Add the garlic from the marinade halfway through cooking. Transfer the beef to a wooden board and rest for 10 minutes before slicing.

Place the Barley Couscous Salad on a serving platter and top with the sliced beef and garlic.

To make your own Couscous see page 281.

Serves 4
- 500g (approx 1lb 2oz) piece sirloin or fillet steak

Marinade
- ½ teaspoon cumin
- ½ teaspoon paprika
- ½ teaspoon ground coriander (cilantro)
- 2 garlic cloves, thinly sliced
- 1 tablespoon extra-virgin olive oil, plus extra for frying (optional)
- sea salt
- freshly ground black pepper

Barley Couscous Salad
- 250g (9oz/1¼ cups) barley couscous or regular couscous or bulghur wheat
- 1 baby cos lettuce, finely chopped
- 1 small handful flat-leaf parsley, finely chopped
- 1 small handful fresh coriander (cilantro), finely chopped
- 1 small handful rocket (arugula)
- 1 small red onion, thinly sliced
- sea salt
- freshly ground black pepper
- 6 tablespoons extra-virgin olive oil
- juice of 1 lemon

Soups

Soup is integral to the Moroccan diet at any
time of the day. Thick Lentil and Bessara (dried
broad bean) soups make filling breakfasts.
Harira, the great Ramadan fast-breaker, is an
enticing mix of chopped lamb, vegetables and
chickpeas, and is a soup that is beloved by all.
There are also some interesting and refreshing
chilled soups, such as Carrot and Orange
sweetened with icing sugar. A chilled soup
makes a delicious starter to any meal.

- 550g (1lb 3oz) carrots, peeled and grated
- 3 tablespoons icing (confectioner's) sugar, plus extra for sprinkling
- 2 tablespoons extra-virgin olive oil, plus extra for drizzling
- 3 tablespoons orange blossom water
- 550ml (18½fl oz/2¼ cups) fresh orange juice

To serve
- cumin salt (see page 261)

Carrot & Orange Soup

Place the carrots, icing sugar, olive oil and orange blossom water in a food processor and blend until smooth. Add the orange juice and blend again briefly to combine the ingredients.

Transfer the mixture to a large bowl, cover with cling film and refrigerate for 1–2 hours.

To serve, ladle the soup into bowls, sprinkle with extra icing sugar, add a drizzle of olive oil and garnish with a pinch of Cumin Salt.

Make your own Cumin Salt. Find the recipe on page 261.

- 3 tablespoons extra-virgin olive oil, plus extra for drizzling
- 1 onion, chopped
- 2 garlic cloves, peeled
- 2kg (4lb 6oz) pumpkin, peeled, deseeded and roughly chopped
- 2 fresh bay leaves
- 1 teaspoon ground cumin
- 1 teaspoon cumin seeds
- small handful flat-leaf parsley
- small handful fresh coriander (cilantro)
- 1 tablespoon saffron threads
- 200g (7oz) tinned chickpeas (garbanzos), drained
- 1.5 litres (48fl oz/approx 6 cups) vegetable stock
- sea salt
- freshly ground black pepper

Spicy Chickpeas
- 100g (3½oz) tinned chickpeas (garbanzos), drained
- ½ tablespoon harissa (see page 267)
- 3 tablespoons extra-virgin olive oil
- squeeze of lemon
- freshly ground black pepper

Pumpkin Soup

To make the Spicy Chickpeas, put all the ingredients in a bowl, season generously with pepper and refrigerate until ready to use.

To make the soup, heat the olive oil in a large saucepan over a medium heat, then add the onion and garlic and sauté until softened. Add the pumpkin, bay leaves, ground cumin, cumin seeds, parsley and coriander and cook for a further 5 minutes, stirring occasionally. Add the saffron threads, chickpeas and vegetable stock. Season generously with salt and pepper, then bring the mixture to the boil. Cover and simmer over a low heat for 40 minutes.

Transfer the soup to a food processor, in batches if necessary, and blend until smooth. Reheat gently and serve in bowls with a drizzle of olive oil and the Spicy Chickpeas on the side.

Bean Soup

Serves 4

Soak **400g (14oz/2 cups) dried haricot beans** in cold water
overnight. Heat **2 tablespoons olive oil** in a large saucepan
over a medium heat, then add **1 large chopped onion** and
1 tablespoon tomato purée and sauté until the onion
is softened. Drain the haricot beans and add to the saucepan.
Add **2 fresh bay leaves** and enough water to just cover the
haricot beans, then bring to the boil, skimming any foam
off the surface with a slotted spoon. Lower the heat and
simmer for 1½ hours or until the beans are tender and
liquid has thickened. Remove and discard the bay leaves.

Transfer 6 tablespoons of beans to a small bowl.
Add **1 tablespoon of olive oil**, **½ tablespoon harissa**
and a pinch of **sea salt** and combine. Set aside until
ready to use.

Add **1 teaspoon cumin** and **½ teaspoon ginger** to the beans
in the saucepan, then transfer the bean mixture, in batches
if necessary, to a food processor and blend until smooth.

Reheat gently, then serve in bowls topped with the bean
mixture and some **Arab-style flatbread** on the side.

Lentil Soup

Serves 4–6

Heat **3 tablespoons extra-virgin olive oil** in a large
saucepan over a medium heat, then add **1 large onion**,
chopped, **1 garlic clove**, chopped, **1 celery stalk, trimmed
and sliced**, and **1 carrot, peeled and diced**, and sauté until
the vegetables are softened.

Add **370g (13oz/approx 1¾ cups) lentils, washed**, and
1.5 litres (48fl oz/approx 6 cups) chicken stock or **water**.
Bring to the boil, cover and simmer over a low heat for about
30 minutes, or until the lentils are tender and beginning to
disintegrate. Add **1 tablespoon ground cumin** and the **juice
of 1 lemon**. Season generously with **sea salt** and **freshly
ground black pepper**. If the soup is too thick, add a little
more water. Garnish with **2 tablespoons finely chopped
coriander (cilantro)** and serve with **crusty bread**.

*Make your own
Moroccan Bread.
See page 282.*

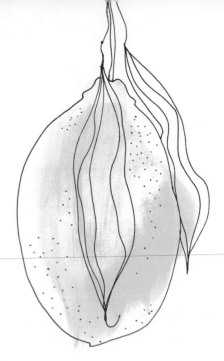

Bessara

This thick soup can be found at market stalls throughout Morocco, and is an early morning breakfast staple.

Serves 4–6

- 300g (10½oz/1½ cups) dried skinned broad beans, soaked overnight
- 4 garlic cloves
- 1 teaspoon dried oregano
- 1 teaspoon ground cumin
- 60ml (2fl oz/¼ cup) extra-virgin olive oil, plus extra for drizzling
- cold water
- sea salt
- freshly ground black pepper

To serve
- lemon wedges

Drain the broad beans and transfer to a large saucepan. Add garlic, oregano, cumin, half the olive oil and enough water to just cover the beans. Bring to the boil, cover and simmer over a low heat for about 1 hour, or until the beans are tender and disintegrating. Remove from the heat and mash to a puréed consistency with a hand blender or potato masher. Add a little extra water if the mixture is too thick. Season generously with salt and pepper and stir in the remaining olive oil. Return soup to pot and reheat gently for 5 minutes.

To serve, ladle the soup into bowls, squeeze over some lemon juice and drizzle with extra olive oil.

Fresh dates and nuts
from the foothills
of the Atlas Mountains

wood carvers

Carved trinkets

dusty hidden alleys

vats of pungent
olive oil

Magic carpets

It's easy to get lost in the maze of souks behind the Djemaa el Fna square. Spices and love charms are sold in the Place Rhaba Kdima (the former slave market square), wood carvings in the Chouari souk, dried fruits and nuts in the Quessabine and Kchacha souks, multi-coloured babouche slippers in the Smata souk, brass and copperware in the Attarine souk and Berber musical instruments in the Kimakhine souk. Just be careful what you buy as they never look as good back home!

Harira Soup

Serves 6
- 2 tablespoons extra virgin olive oil
- 2 onions, peeled and finely chopped
- 3 garlic cloves, peeled and finely chopped
- 2 celery stalks, trimmed and finely chopped
- 2 carrots, peeled and finely chopped
- 1 tablespoon flat-leaf parsley, finely chopped
- 500g (1lb 2oz) leg of lamb, cut into 1cm (½in) pieces
- 1 tablespoon ground cumin
- 2 tablespoons ground turmeric
- 2 tablespoons paprika
- 1 tablespoon cinnamon
- 2 fresh bay leaves
- 1 tablespoon tomato pureé
- 1 litre vegetable stock
- 400g (14oz) can chopped tomatoes
- 400g (14oz) chickpeas (garbanzos), drained
- sea salt
- freshly ground black pepper

To serve
- Arab-style flatbread

This famous soup is traditionally eaten at sundown to break the fast each day during the thirty fasting days of Ramadan, when it is commonly served with dates and honey cakes called grioche. There are many versions of this nourishing soup with or without meat and using different pulses such as chickpeas and lentils.

Heat olive oil in a large saucepan over medium heat and sauté the onion, garlic, celery, carrots and parsley for about 5–7 minutes or until softened. Add the lamb and brown, stirring, for about 5 minutes.

Next add the cumin, turmeric, paprika, cinnamon, bay leaves and tomato purée, stir well and cook for 5 minutes. Add stock, bring to the boil then lower the heat and simmer, covered, for 1 hour or until the meat is tender.

Add the tomatoes and chickpeas and cook for a further 30 minutes, adding a little more water if the mixture is too thick. Season generously with salt and pepper then ladle into bowls and serve with bread.

Moroccan Bread with this soup would be great. See how to make your own on page 282

Chorba

- 2 tablespoons extra-virgin olive oil, plus extra for drizzling
- 1 medium red onion, diced
- 1 large potato, peeled and diced
- 2 large carrots, peeled and diced
- 3 large courgettes (zucchinis), sliced and diced
- 1 celery heart, trimmed and chopped
- 1 tablespoon fresh coriander (cilantro), finely chopped
- 400g (14oz) tinned cherry tomatoes
- 1 teaspoon saffron threads
- 1.5 litres (48fl oz/approx 6 cups) vegetable stock
- 1 teaspoon ground coriander (cilantro)
- 100g (3½oz) tinned chickpeas (garbanzos), drained
- sea salt
- freshly ground black pepper
- 250g (9oz) vermicelli
- ½ small preserved lemon, flesh removed, rind sliced (see page 253)

To serve
- juice of ½ lemon
- spicy chickpeas, (see page 115)

Heat the olive oil in a large saucepan over a medium heat, then add the onion and sauté until softened. Add the potato, carrots, courgettes, celery and fresh coriander and cook, stirring occasionally, for a further 5 minutes. Add the cherry tomatoes, saffron threads, vegetable stock, ground coriander and chickpeas and season generously with salt and pepper.

Bring the mixture to the boil, then add the vermicelli. Cover and simmer over a low heat for 40 minutes. Just before serving, add the preserved lemon rind.

To serve, ladle the soup into bowls, squeeze over some lemon juice and accompany with Spicy Chickpeas on the side.

Reheat gently, then serve in bowls with the Spicy Chickpeas on the side, and a drizzle of olive oil.

Chicken & Fennel Soup

Place all stock ingredients in a large saucepan. Add cold water until just covered, then bring to the boil over medium heat, skimming any foam off the surface with a slotted spoon. Reduce the heat to low, cover and simmer for 2 hours.

Remove from the heat and allow to cool before transferring the chicken to a large bowl. Strain the stock through a fine colander into a large bowl, discard the remaining ingredients, then transfer the stock back to the saucepan.

Remove the bones and skin from the chicken and roughly shred the chicken meat back into the saucepan with the stock. Add the fennel seeds and baby fennel and bring to the boil over a medium heat.

Place the tomato purée in a small bowl, add a couple of tablespoons of the chicken stock and mix to dissolve the tomato purée. Add the tomato mixture and the orzo to the soup. Simmer over a low heat for 15–18 minutes, or until the orzo is cooked.

Serve in bowls with a sprinkling of flat-leaf parsley, a small dollop of harissa, a drizzle of olive oil and bread rolls on the side.

Serves 6
- 1 teaspoon fennel seeds
- 4 baby fennel bulbs, including green tops, finely diced
- 1 tablespoon tomato purée
- 400g (14oz) orzo

Stock
- 1.5kg (3lb) chicken
- 1 bulb fennel, trimmed and chopped
- 1 onion, halved
- 4 garlic cloves, crushed
- 1 carrot, roughly chopped
- 1 small handful flat-leaf parsley
- 3 celery sticks, trimmed and roughly chopped
- 1 tablespoon black peppercorns
- 1 tablespoon white peppercorns
- 3 fresh bay leaves
- cold water

To serve
- 4 tablespoons flat-leaf parsley, finely chopped
- 1 tablespoon harissa (see page 267)
- extra-virgin olive oil, for drizzling
- bread rolls, halved

Fish Soup

Heat the olive oil in a large saucepan over medium heat, then add the onion, celery and garlic and sauté until softened. Add the ginger, harissa, coriander seeds and parsley and cook for 5 minutes, stirring occasionally. Season with salt and pepper, then add the tomatoes and cook for a further 5 minutes.

Add the fish stock or water and bring to the boil. Lower the heat, cover and simmer for 10 minutes.

Add the fish, prawns and squid and cook for 15 minutes, or until all the seafood is cooked through.

Just before serving, add lemon juice, then ladle into soup bowls and serve with bread on the side.

Serves 4
- 2 tablespoons extra-virgin olive oil
- 1 medium red onion, thinly sliced
- 1 celery stalk, trimmed and sliced
- 2 garlic cloves, thinly sliced
- ½ teaspoon ground ginger
- ½ tablespoon harissa (see page 267)
- ½ tablespoon coriander (cilantro) seeds, crushed
- 3 tablespoons flat-leaf parsley, finely chopped
- sea salt
- freshly ground black pepper
- 2 ripe tomatoes, peeled and chopped
- 500ml (17fl oz/2 cups) fish stock or water
- 1kg (2lb) fish, such as snapper, cod, sea bass, cut into chunks
- 8 king prawns, cleaned with tails on
- 250g (9oz) squid, cleaned and sliced
- juice of 1 lemon

To serve
- crusty bread

Harissa would be great with this soup. See how to make your own on page 267.

Savoury Pastries

The wonderfully robust and light warkha pastry is seen in every Moroccan market and food store. There's a host of easy and inventive baked and fried recipes for Briouats and Briks in all shapes and sizes – filo pastry makes a good substitute if you can't find warkha. The pièce de resistance of all these recipes is the Bistilla – a layered pie filled with an aromatic and rich spice-scented mixture of pigeon, chicken or quail, dusted with icing sugar and cinnamon. Bistilla is always a part of any Moroccan feast.

Vegetable Briouat

To make the dip, mix the harissa, yoghurt and olive oil in a serving bowl and set aside until ready to use.

Preheat the oven to 170°C (340°F). To make the filling, place the tomatoes, courgettes, onion, garlic, peppers, and aubergine in a roasting tin. Season generously with salt and pepper, then add the olive oil and Ras el Hanout and combine well.

Roast the vegetables for 1½ hours until they are cooked and nicely browned. Remove from the oven, allow to cool, then chop all the vegetables again into small pieces. Add the lemon juice, an extra drizzle of olive oil and the parsley and toss to combine.

To make the briouats, take one sheet of warkha pastry and place a quarter of the filling mixture all along one side of the pastry. Roll up the pastry to form a long cigar shape, then cut off any excess pastry beyond the vegetable filling. Repeat four times.

Fill a large frying pan a third full with olive oil, then place over a medium heat. When hot, carefully drop the briouats into the pan and fry for about 5–7 minutes, turning until the pastry is golden brown on all sides. Depending on the size of your frying pan, you may need to fry the briouats in batches.

Serve immediately with the Harissa Yoghurt Dip and a wedge of lemon.

Note If using filo pastry, which tends to be a large rectangular shape, cut the eight sheets in half. For each briouat, use four cut sheets of filo. After you have rolled the briouats, moisten the edges with a little melted butter or olive oil to make the pastry stick together.

Serves 4
- 4 sheets warkha pastry, or 8 sheets filo pastry
- olive oil for frying

Filling
- 4 ripe tomatoes, halved
- 4 courgettes (zucchinis), chopped
- 1 brown onion, peeled and roughly chopped
- 3 cloves garlic, peeled and squashed
- 1 red pepper (capsicum), deseeded and roughly chopped
- 1 green pepper (capsicum), deseeded and roughly chopped
- 1 aubergine (eggplant), halved and sliced
- sea salt
- freshly ground black pepper
- 4 tablespoons extra-virgin olive oil, plus extra for drizzling
- 1 tablespoon ras el hanout (see page 258)
- juice of ½ lemon
- 2 tablespoons flat-leaf parsley

Harissa Yoghurt Dip
- 1 tablespoon harissa (see page 267)
- 8 tablespoons thick Greek-style yoghurt
- 1 tablespoon extra-virgin olive oil

To serve
- lemon wedges

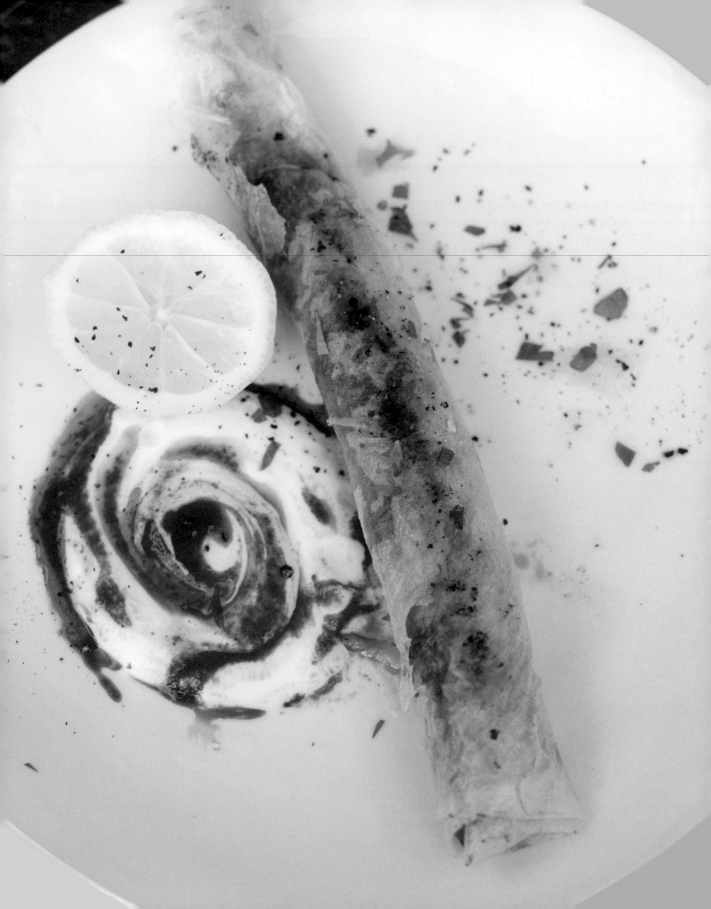

Find the recipe for Harissa on page 267.

Serves 6
- 1 tablespoon extra-virgin olive oil, plus extra for frying
- 6 Merguez sausages
- 3 sheets warkha pastry, or 6 sheets filo pastry
- 1 tablespoon harissa, plus extra for drizzling (see page 267)

Merguez Briouat

These cigar-shaped pastries are like a Moroccan sausage roll. They are simple to make and a great canapé to serve with drinks. Once cooked, simply cut them in half for a party-sized platter.

Heat the olive oil in a frying pan over a medium heat and cook the Merguez sausages, turning occasionally, for about 5 minutes or until cooked. Transfer to a plate lined with kitchen paper.

Take a sheet of warkha pastry and cut in half. Smear a little harissa in the middle and add a Merguez sausage about 1cm (½in) in from one of the edges. Roll up tightly like a cigar, then cut off any excess pastry beyond the Merguez sausage filling. Repeat the process with the remaining ingredients to make three briouats.

When hot, carefully drop two or three briouats into the pan and fry for about 3–5 minutes, turning until the pastry is golden brown on all sides. Repeat the process with the remaining briouats.

Serve immediately with an extra drizzle of harissa.

Note If using filo pastry, which tends to be a rectangular shape when unfolded, cut the sheets in half to form two large rectangles. For each briouat, use two sheets of filo. Brush each sheet of pastry with melted butter or olive oil.

Lamb & Artichoke Briouat

If fresh artichokes are unavailable, simply use good quality ones from a tin or a jar, and drain them before combining with the other ingredients.

To make the filling, combine the lamb, artichokes, preserved lemon, cumin and olive oil in a bowl. Season generously with salt and pepper and mix well.

To make the briouats, take a sheet of warkha pastry and cut in half. Place one-sixth of the lamb filling about 1cm (½in) in along one of the edges. Roll up tightly like a cigar, then cut off any excess pastry beyond the lamb filling. Repeat process with the remaining ingredients to make three briouats.

Fill a large frying pan with enough olive oil to come one-third of the way up the sides, then heat the oil over a medium heat. When hot, carefully drop two or three briouats into the pan and fry for 3–5 minutes, turning until the pastry is golden brown on all sides. Repeat the process with the remaining briouats. Cut them in half and serve immediately with a squeeze of preserved or fresh lemon juice.

Note If using filo pastry, which tends to be a rectangular shape when unfolded, cut the sheets in half to form two large rectangles. For each briouat, use two sheets of filo. Brush each sheet of pastry with melted butter or olive oil.

Serves 6
- 220g (8oz) cooked lamb, shredded
- 2 cooked fresh/tinned artichoke hearts, roughly chopped
- 1 small preserved lemon, roughly chopped (see page 253)
- 1 teaspoon ground cumin
- 1 tablespoon extra-virgin olive oil, plus extra for frying
- sea salt
- freshly ground black pepper
- 3 sheets warkha pastry or 6 sheets filo pastry

To serve
- half a preserved lemon, or fresh lemon

Marrakesh Fabric Dyeing

Texture

Fuchsia

Wool

RoofTops

Ultramarine

Lemon

Vibrant

Crimson

Golden

Azure

The dyers' market in the Souk Sebbaghine is best seen from the terraces above some of the stores that sell dyes and pigments. From here, you can see a riot of colourful textiles and dyed cloths drying in the sun. In the alleys below, there are huge cauldrons of natural pigment dyes, such as rose petals, mallow, pomegranate, poppy, cobalt, saffron and indigo, which the raw materials are plunged into by the workers as they pose for the tourist hordes.

Kefta Briks with Herb Dip

4 (makes 16 Briks)
- 4 sheets warkha pastry or 16 sheets filo pastry

Filling
- 2 tablespoons extra-virgin olive oil
- 350g (12oz) minced (ground) lamb
- 1 small red onion, finely grated
- 2 garlic cloves, peeled and finely chopped
- 1 teaspoon ground cumin
- 1 teaspoon paprika
- ½ teaspoon ground cinnamon
- ½ teaspoon ground ginger
- 1 tablespoon fresh coriander (cilantro), finely chopped
- 1 tablespoon mint, finely chopped
- olive oil, for frying

Herb Dip
- 1 small handful rocket (arugula)
- 4 tablespoons fresh mint
- 4 tablespoons flat-leaf parsley
- 4 tablespoons fresh coriander (cilantro)
- 4 tablespoons chives
- 4 tablespoons extra-virgin olive oil
- sea salt
- freshly ground black pepper

To make the Herb Dip, place the herbs in a food processor and blend to a rough paste. Slowly incorporate the olive oil, then transfer to a bowl. Season with salt and pepper, cover with cling film and set aside until ready to use.

For the filling, heat the olive oil in a frying pan over a medium heat, then add the minced lamb and brown, stirring occasionally, for 5 minutes. Transfer to a plate. Add the onion and garlic to the pan and sauté for 3–4 minutes until softened. Add the cumin, paprika, cinnamon, ginger, coriander and mint and stir for a few minutes. Return the minced lamb to the pan and cook, stirring occasionally, for about 10 minutes. Transfer to a bowl and set aside to cool.

To make the briks, take a sheet of warkha pastry and cut in half to create two rectangles 10 x 10cm (4 x 4in) in size. Take one cut sheet of pastry and fold over each of the longer edges about 4cm (2in). Put a tablespoon of filling in the corner at one of the shorter ends. Fold the pastry over into a triangle, then continue folding until you reach the other end and have a finished triangle shaped briks. Repeat the process with the remaining ingredients to make sixteen briks.

Fill a large frying pan a third full with olive oil, then place over a medium heat. When hot, carefully drop two or three briks into the pan and fry for 3–5 minutes, turning, until the pastry is golden brown on all sides. Repeat the process with the remaining briks and serve immediately with the Herb Dip.

Note If using filo pastry, which tends to be a rectangular shape when unfolded, cut the sixteen sheets of filo into three 12 x 28cm (5 x 11in) strips. Use three strips of pastry per brik, and brush each strip with a little melted butter or olive oil.

Goat's Cheese & Herb Brik

To make the filling, place the goat's cheese or fromage frais, fresh herbs, beaten egg, ground cumin, olive oil and lemon juice in a bowl. Season generously with salt and pepper and mix well.

To make the brik, lay a sheet of warkha on a flat surface and cut a 20cm (8in) circle. If using filo pastry, place two sheets on a flat surface and discard any remaining filo pastry. Place half the goat's cheese and herb filling in the centre of the pastry. Fold the pastry edges into the centre to enclose the filling, then invert onto a surface lightly dusted with flour. Repeat the process with the remaining ingredients to make a second brik.

Fill a large frying pan a third full with olive oil, then place over a medium heat. Add one brik and cook for about 4–5 minutes, or until golden brown. Remove and place on kitchen paper. Cook the remaining brik in the same way.

Serve immediately with a squeeze of lemon juice.

Serves 2
- 2 sheets warkha pastry or 4 sheets filo pastry
- a little plain (all-purpose) flour, for dusting
- olive oil, for frying

Filling
- 250g (9oz) soft goat's cheese or fromage frais
- 1 bunch mixed fresh herbs, such as flat-leaf parsley, basil, mint, chives, dill and coriander (cilantro), finely chopped
- 1 egg, beaten
- ½ teaspoon ground cumin
- 2 tablespoons extra-virgin olive oil
- juice of 1 lemon
- sea salt
- freshly ground black pepper

To serve
- half a lemon

Chicken & Tomato Brik

To make the filling, heat the olive oil in a frying pan over a medium heat, then add the onion and sauté until softened. Stir in the cumin, ginger and cinnamon and season generously with salt and pepper. Add the tomato and cook, stirring occasionally, for 5 minutes or until softened. Stir in the chicken and cook for a further 2 minutes. Transfer to a bowl, allow to cool for 5 minutes, then add the egg and combine well.

To make the brik, take a sheet of warkha pastry and fold the sides in about 4cm (1½in) to make a 18 x 18cm (7 x 7in) square. Place a quarter of the filling in the centre of a pastry square, then fold the pastry over to form a triangle. Repeat the process with the remaining ingredients so you have four briks.

Fill a large frying pan a third full with olive oil, then place over a medium heat. When hot, carefully drop the briks into the pan and fry for about 5–7 minutes, turning once, until the pastry is golden brown. Depending on the size of your frying pan, you may need to fry the brik in batches. Once all the briks have been fried serve immediately with yoghurt on the side.

Note If using filo pastry, which tends to be a large rectangular shape, cut the eight sheets in half. For each brik, take a stack of four cut sheets and fold them in half to form a square. Make the brik as you do when using warkha pastry, but moisten the edges with a little melted butter or olive oil to make them stick together.

Serves 4 (makes 4 Briks)
- 4 sheets warkha pastry or 8 sheets filo pastry
- olive oil, for frying

Filling
- 2 tablespoons extra-virgin olive oil
- 1 medium onion, roughly chopped
- 1 teaspoon ground cumin
- 1 teaspoon ground ginger
- 1 teaspoon ground cinnamon
- sea salt
- freshly ground black pepper
- 1 tomato, peeled and roughly chopped
- 220g (8oz) cooked chicken, shredded
- 1 egg, beaten

To serve
- thick Greek-style yoghurt

Crab Brik

To make the filling, place the crab, onion, harissa, cumin, parsley, olive oil and lemon juice in a bowl. Season generously with salt and pepper and mix well.

To make the brik, lay a sheet of warkha pastry on a flat surface and cut out a 20cm (8in) circle. If using filo pastry, place 2 sheets on a flat surface and discard any remaining filo pastry. Place half of the crab filling in the centre of the pastry. Fold the pastry edges into the centre to enclose the filling, then invert onto a surface lightly dusted with flour. Repeat the process with the remaining ingredients to make a second brik.

Fill a large frying pan a third full with olive oil, then place over a medium heat. Add one brik and cook for about 4–5 minutes or until golden brown. Remove and place on kitchen paper. Cook the remaining brik in the same way, then serve immediately with a squeeze of lemon juice.

Serves 2
- 2 sheets warkha pastry or 4 sheets filo pastry
- a little plain (all-purpose) flour, for dusting
- olive oil, for frying

Filling
- 160g (5½oz) crab meat
- ½ red onion, peeled and finely chopped
- 1 teaspoon harissa (see page 267)
- ½ teaspoon ground cumin
- 2 tablespoons flat-leaf parsley, finely chopped
- 1 tablespoon extra-virgin olive oil
- 1 tablespoon lemon juice
- sea salt
- freshly ground black pepper

To serve
- ½ a lemon

Serves 6–8

- 2 tablespoons extra-virgin olive oil
- 1 medium red onion, thinly sliced
- 2 cloves garlic, finely sliced
- 1½ teaspoons saffron threads
- 1 teaspoon quatre épices
- 1 teaspoon ground ginger
- 1 teaspoon ground coriander (cilantro)
- 1 teaspoon ground cinnamon
- ½ teaspoon ground nutmeg
- 400ml (13fl oz/approx 1¾ cups) chicken stock, warmed
- 2 eggs, beaten
- 800g (1lb 12oz) cooked chicken, shredded
- 50g (2oz/⅓ cup) sultanas, soaked in warm water
- 80g (3oz/approx 1 cup) almonds, chopped
- juice of 1 orange
- sea salt
- freshly ground black pepper
- 50g (2oz/approx ½ stick) butter, melted for brushing (plus extra 150g/5oz/1 stick if using filo pastry)
- 8 sheets warkha pastry or 12 sheets filo pastry
- icing (confectioner's) sugar, for dusting

To serve
- green salad

Chicken Bistilla

Heat the olive oil in a large saucepan over a medium heat, then add the onion and garlic and sauté until softened. Add the saffron threads, quatre épices, ginger, coriander, cinnamon and nutmeg and cook, stirring continuously, for 2–3 minutes. Add the chicken stock and bring to the boil, then lower the heat and simmer for 10 minutes until the sauce has thickened and the liquid has reduced by half.

Remove from the heat, then add the eggs, shredded chicken, sultanas, almonds, orange juice and stir well. Allow to cool, then season with salt and pepper.

Preheat the oven to 180°C (350°F) and lightly grease a 22cm (8½in) pie dish. If using filo pastry, brush the pastry sheets with the melted butter and stack them on top of each other.

Place four sheets of overlapping warkha pastry, or six sheets of filo pastry, on the bottom of the prepared pie dish. Spoon in the chicken mixture, then top with the remaining warkha or filo pastry sheets. Pull the edges of the pastry away from rim of pie dish, so that they crimp up a little during baking. Brush the top of the bistilla with melted butter. Bake in the oven for 20–30 minutes, or until the pastry is golden.

Remove from the oven and cool for 3 minutes before transferring to a serving plate. Dust with icing sugar and serve sliced with a simple fresh green salad.

Pigeon Bistilla

This is one of the most famous dishes you'll find in Morocco. Traditionally, it is made with pigeon, although many restaurants make it with chicken these days to cater for more squeamish tourist tastes.

Heat the olive oil in a large saucepan over a medium heat, then add the onion and garlic and sauté until softened. Add the pigeon and all the Chermoula ingredients, and cook for 3–5 minutes, stirring continuously.

Add the chicken stock or water and bring to the boil. Lower the heat and simmer for 50–60 minutes, or until the pigeon is tender and the sauce is beginning to thicken. Transfer the pigeon pieces to a plate with a slotted spoon. Allow to cool, then remove the bones and roughly shred the pigeon meat into a large bowl.

Meanwhile, cook the sauce over a high heat until it reduces by about half and thickens. Allow to cool, then add the shredded pigeon meat, eggs and almonds. Season generously with salt and pepper. Stir until well combined.

Preheat the oven to 180°C (350°F) and lightly grease a 26cm (10in) pie dish. If using filo pastry, brush the pastry sheets with melted butter and stack them on top of each other with the edges overlapping. Place four sheets of overlapping warkha pastry, or six sheets of filo pastry, on the bottom of the prepared pie dish, making sure the edges overhang the rim. Spoon in half the pigeon mixture, then layer the centre of the pie dish with the remaining warkha or filo pastry sheets. Add the remaining pigeon mixture, and then fold the overhanging pastry neatly into the centre. Brush the top of the bistilla with melted butter. Bake in the oven for 20–30 minutes, or until the pastry is golden.

Remove from the oven and cool for 3 minutes before transferring to a serving plate. Dust with icing sugar and cinnamon and serve sliced.

Serves 6–8

- 2 tablespoons extra-virgin olive oil
- 1 medium onion, thinly sliced
- 2 cloves garlic, finely sliced
- 5 pigeons, quartered
- 400ml (13fl oz/1¾ cups) chicken stock or water
- 2 eggs, beaten
- 80g (3oz/approx 1 cup) almonds, chopped
- sea salt
- freshly ground black pepper
- 8 sheets warkha pastry or 12 sheets filo pastry
- 50g (2oz/approx ½ stick) butter, melted for brushing (plus extra 150g/5oz/1 stick if using filo pastry)
- butter, for brushing

Chermoula
- 1½ teaspoons saffron threads
- ½ teaspoon ground turmeric
- 1 teaspoon ground ginger
- 1 teaspoon ground coriander (cilantro)
- 1 teaspoon ground cinnamon
- ½ teaspoon ground nutmeg

To serve
- icing (confectioner's) sugar, for dusting
- ground cinnamon, for dusting

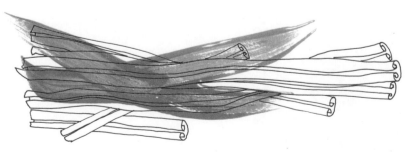

Tagines

I'm not sure where Moroccan cooking would be without its tagines. They are the very heart and soul of its cuisine – simple one-pot meat, fish or vegetable stews simmered with fruits, herbs and spices that are eaten on a daily basis with mounds of steaming couscous. Easy to make, they also help define the communal dining that is so intrinsic to Moroccan family life, where dishes are put in the centre of the table for everyone to tuck into.

Serves 6

- 300g (10½oz) chickpeas (garbanzos), soaked in water overnight
- cold water
- extra-virgin olive oil, for drizzling
- 8 large carrots, peeled and halved lengthways
- 8 small onions, peeled whole
- 2 large potatoes, peeled and cut lengthways into thick pieces
- 1kg (2lb 3oz) pumpkin, peeled and cut into thick pieces
- 600g (1lb 5oz) cabbage, cut into thick pieces
- 6 medium courgettes (zucchinis), trimmed and halved lengthways
- 8 small round aubergines (eggplants), halved
- sea salt
- freshly ground black pepper

Couscous

- 500g (1lb 2oz/2½ cups) couscous
- cold water
- 5 tablespoons extra-virgin olive oil, plus extra for drizzling
- sea salt
- 1 teaspoon ground saffron
- 1 teaspoon ground ginger
- 2 tablespoons flat-leaf parsley, including stems, finely chopped
- 1 tablespoon tomato purée
- freshly ground black pepper
- 180g (6oz/1½ sticks) unsalted butter

To serve

- harissa (see page 267)

Sept Legumes with Couscous

In a grander version, known as Couscous Royale, popular throughout the Mahgreb and Parisian restaurants, this dish is cooked with different meats, such as lamb and Merguez sausages, but a vegetarian version is just as good. Traditionally, the seven vegetables used are potatoes, carrots, pumpkin, courgettes, turnips, cabbage and onions, but you can add what you like.

Drain the chickpeas and remove any skins. Place in a large saucepan, cover with water and cook over a medium heat for 1½ hours, or until tender. Drain, transfer to a bowl and drizzle with olive oil.

Place the couscous in a large bowl, cover with cold water and mix well. Drain immediately and place the couscous back in the bowl, then leave for 10 minutes. Rub the grains together between your hands, letting them fall back into the bowl, to break up any lumps. Leave for a further 10 minutes. Add 3 tablespoons of the olive oil, a pinch of salt and about 100ml (3½fl oz) cold water and mix until all the liquid is absorbed.

Place the saffron, ginger, parsley, tomato purée, remaining olive oil and 3.5 litres (119fl oz) of water in the bottom of the couscoussier. Season with salt and pepper. Bring to the boil over a medium heat. Add the couscous into the top part of the couscoussier, cover with lid and steam for 30 minutes.

Remove the couscoussier from the heat and transfer couscous to the bowl. Allow to cool then mix in one-third of the butter with your hands. Then, slowly add 300ml (10fl oz) cold water combining it with the couscous grains. Return couscous to the top part of the couscoussier, replace the lid, and steam over the boiling liquid for 20 minutes. Transfer couscous back into the bowl, allow to cool then add another third of the butter and mix with your hands.

Meanwhile, add carrots, onions and potatoes to the liquid in the bottom of couscoussier and cook for about 5 minutes over a low heat. Add chickpeas, pumpkin, cabbage, courgettes and aubergines to the other vegetables in the couscoussier.

Return the couscous back to the top part of couscoussier, cover with the lid. Simmer the vegetables and chickpeas, and steam couscous over a low heat for 20 minutes, or until the vegetables are tender.

Remove the couscoussier from the heat and transfer the couscous to the bowl again. Allow to cool then add remaining butter and mix, using your hands.

Transfer couscous to a serving bowl. Using a slotted spoon, arrange the vegetables and chickpeas over the couscous. Pour some liquid from the couscoussier over the vegetables and serve with harissa.

Potato, Fennel & Pea Tagine

Heat the olive oil over a medium heat in a casserole dish or tagine. Add the potatoes, onion and garlic and cook for 2–3 minutes. Add celery and fennel and cook for a further 2–3 minutes.

Add the ginger, coriander and cumin and season generously with salt and pepper, then add the peas and enough water to just cover the mixture. Bring to the boil, then lower the heat, cover with the lid and simmer for 15 minutes, or until the vegetables are tender.

Add the parsley and mint, and remove the lid. Cook for 10 minutes or until the sauce reduces and thickens, stirring to prevent it from sticking to the pan.

Lastly, add the lemon juice, drizzle with olive oil and serve with couscous.

Serves 4
- 2 tablespoons extra-virgin olive oil, plus extra for drizzling
- 400g (14oz) baby potatoes, cleaned
- 1 onion, peeled and chopped
- 4 cloves garlic, thinly sliced
- 2 celery sticks, trimmed and sliced
- 2 bulbs fennel, trimmed and sliced lengthways
- 1 teaspoon ground ginger
- ½ teaspoon ground coriander (cilantro)
- ½ teaspoon ground cumin
- sea salt
- freshly ground black pepper
- 250g (9oz) shelled fresh or frozen peas
- cold water
- 1½ tablespoons flat-leaf parsley, finely chopped
- 1½ tablespoons mint, finely chopped

To serve
- couscous (see page 281)
- juice of 1 lemon

Kefta, Tomato & Egg Tagine

For the kefta, combine the minced beef or lamb, red onion, cumin, paprika, ground coriander, ground ginger and fresh coriander in a large bowl. Season generously with salt and pepper, then mix well and shape into 3cm (1in) balls.

Heat the olive oil in a large frying pan over a medium heat and sauté the kefta for about 5–7 minutes, browning on all sides. Transfer the kefta to a plate.

To make the Tomato Sauce, add the onion, garlic and parsley to the frying pan over a medium heat and sauté for 5 minutes until softened. Add the tomatoes, cumin, and cinnamon and season generously with salt and pepper. Add a little water, stir and cook for 5 minutes.

Return the kefta to the frying pan with the sauce and cook for 30 minutes, or until the sauce has reduced and thickened.

Make four little indentations in the top of the sauce, then break eggs carefully into them. Continue to cook for about 3–5 minutes or until eggs have set.

Serve immediately with some parsley sprinkled over the top.

Serves 4
Kefta
- 500g (1lb 2oz) minced beef or lamb
- 1 small red onion, finely grated
- ½ teaspoon ground cumin
- ½ teaspoon paprika
- ½ teaspoon ground coriander (cilantro)
- ½ teaspoon ground ginger, finely grated
- 1 tablespoon fresh coriander (cilantro), finely chopped
- sea salt
- freshly ground black pepper
- 2 tablespoons extra-virgin olive oil
- 4 eggs

Tomato Sauce
- 1 large onion, chopped
- 3 cloves garlic, finely chopped
- 1 small bunch flat-leaf parsley, finely chopped, plus extra for sprinkling
- 1kg (2lb 3oz) tomatoes, peeled, deseeded and chopped
- ½ tablespoon ground cumin
- ½ teaspoon ground cinnamon
- sea salt
- freshly ground black pepper
- cold water

Rabbit, Turnip & Carrot Tagine

Place the rabbit pieces in a large bowl. Add the ginger, saffron, coriander, cinnamon stick, rosemary, parsley and half the olive oil, and rub into the rabbit pieces. Cover with cling film and refrigerate for 1–2 hours.

Remove the rabbit from the refrigerator. Heat the remaining olive oil in a casserole dish or tagine on a medium setting. Add the rabbit pieces, reserving any of the remaining marinade, and brown for 5 minutes. Transfer the rabbit pieces to a plate.

Add the onions, garlic, carrots, turnips, tomatoes, tomato purée and remaining marinade to the casserole dish and sauté for 5 minutes.

Return the rabbit pieces to the casserole dish and add enough water to just cover the mixture. Bring to the boil, then lower the heat and simmer for 1½ hours, or until the meat and vegetables are tender and the sauce has thickened.

Serve with couscous or crusty bread.

Serves 4
- 1 x 750g (1lb 10oz) rabbit, jointed into 6 pieces
- 1 teaspoon ground ginger
- 1 teaspoon saffron threads
- 1 teaspoon ground coriander (cilantro)
- 1 cinnamon stick
- ½ tablespoon fresh rosemary leaves
- 1 tablespoon flat-leaf parsley, finely chopped
- 4 tablespoons extra-virgin olive oil
- 4 small onions, peeled and quartered
- 2 cloves garlic, sliced
- 12 small carrots, peeled whole
- 12 baby turnips, trimmed
- 2 plum tomatoes, sliced
- 3 tablespoons tomato purée
- cold water

To serve
- couscous (see page 281) or crusty bread

Make your own Couscous. See page 281.

brick red

Tagines

charcoal burning braziers

Clay

olive green bowls

flowerpots

POTERIE MARRA

Beyond the tanneries, there's a string of pottery workshops where locals come to buy their garden pots, ceramic bowls, earthenware tagines and charcoal-burning braziers in all shapes and sizes. They're a fraction of the price you pay in the Medina souks and a refreshing detour after the pungent smells of the tanneries.

Fish & Fennel Tagine

To make the Chermoula, place garlic, cumin, cayenne pepper, paprika, saffron, chilli, parsley and coriander in a food processor. Season with salt and pepper, then blend until well combined. Add the olive oil and lemon juice and blend to a paste. Transfer to a large bowl.

Add the fish to the Chermoula and gently toss until well coated. Cover with cling film and refrigerate for 30 minutes.

Meanwhile, heat the olive oil in a large casserole dish, or tagine, over a medium heat. Add the onion and sauté for 5 minutes until softened, then add the fennel and sauté for a further 5 minutes, or until softened. Add the cherry tomatoes and cook for 5 minutes, then pour in the fish stock and bring to the boil. Lower the heat and simmer for 10 minutes.

Add the fish to the casserole dish and stir the mixture well. Cover and simmer for 10–12 minutes or until the fish is cooked and the sauce has thickened.

Serve immediately with couscous.

Serves 6
- 2kg (4lb 6oz) thick fish fillets, such as cod, cut into pieces
- 3 tablespoons extra-virgin olive oil
- 1 red onion, peeled and sliced
- 160g (5½oz) baby fennel, trimmed and sliced lengthways
- 400g (14oz) tinned cherry tomatoes
- 200ml (7fl oz/approx ¾ cup) fish stock

Chermoula
- 3 garlic cloves, finely chopped
- 1 teaspoon ground cumin
- ½ teaspoon cayenne pepper
- ½ teaspoon paprika
- 1 teaspoon saffron
- 1 red chilli, deseeded and sliced
- 2 tablespoons flat-leaf parsley, finely chopped
- 2 tablespoons fresh coriander (cilantro), finely chopped
- sea salt
- freshly ground black pepper
- 4 tablespoons extra-virgin olive oil
- juice of ½ lemon

To serve
- couscous (see page 281)

Serves 4

- 1.5–2kg (3–4lb) snapper (or other firm-fleshed fish), cleaned and cut into fillets
- 3 tablespoons extra-virgin olive oil
- 2 red onions, thinly sliced
- 3 ripe tomatoes, peeled, deseeded and roughly chopped
- 200ml (7fl oz/approx ¾ cup) fish stock
- 200g (7oz/1⅓ cup) green olives, drained
- 1 preserved lemon, roughly chopped (see page 253)

Harissa Spiced Chermoula
- 3 garlic cloves, finely chopped
- 1 teaspoon ground cumin
- ½ teaspoon cayenne pepper
- ½ teaspoon paprika
- 1 teaspoon saffron threads
- ½ tablespoon harissa (see page 267)
- 1 small red chilli, deseeded and chopped
- 2 tablespoons flat-leaf parsley, finely chopped
- 2 tablespoons fresh coriander (cilantro), finely chopped
- sea salt
- freshly ground black pepper
- 4 tablespoons extra-virgin olive oil
- juice of ½ lemon

To serve
- couscous (see page 281)

Make your own Preserved lemons. See page 253.

Snapper, Green Olives & Preserved Lemon Tagine

To make the Harissa Spiced Chermoula, place garlic, cumin, cayenne pepper, paprika, saffron, harissa, chilli, parsley and coriander in a food processor. Season with salt and pepper, then blend until well combined. Add olive oil and lemon juice and blend to a paste. Transfer to a large bowl.

Slice each of the snapper fillets into three or four pieces. Add the snapper to the bowl of Harissa Spiced Chermoula, then gently toss until well coated. Cover and refrigerate for 30 minutes. Meanwhile, heat the olive oil in a large casserole dish, or tagine, over a medium heat. Add the onions and sauté for 5 minutes until softened, then add the tomatoes and cook for 5 minutes. Add the fish stock and bring to the boil, then lower the heat and simmer for 10 minutes.

Add the fish pieces, olives and preserved lemon to the casserole dish and stir the mixture well. Cover and simmer for 10 minutes, or until the fish is cooked and the sauce has thickened.

Serve immediately with couscous.

Baby Octopus & Green Olive Tagine

Serves 4–6

Heat **4 tablespoons extra-virgin olive oil** in a large saucepan over medium heat, then add **1kg (2lb) baby octopus, cleaned**, **4 small onions, peeled and thinly sliced**, and **2 cloves garlic, peeled and thinly sliced** and sauté for 5–7 minutes, or until softened. Add **1 tablespoon flat-leaf parsley, finely chopped**, **1 tablespoon tomato purée**, **½ teaspoon ras el hanout (see page 258)**, **½ tablespoon ground ginger**, **1 teaspoon paprika**, **1 teaspoon ground cumin** and **1 teaspoon coriander (cilantro) seeds** and cook for 5 minutes, stirring continuously. Add **water** to just cover the mixture, then simmer over a low heat, covered, for 45 minutes, or until the octopus is tender and the sauce has thickened. Add **100g (3½oz/⅔ cups) green olives, drained and stoned**, during last 20 minutes of cooking. Serve immediately with **Arab-style flatbread**.

Prawn & Tomato Tagine

Serves 4

Cut a cross in the top of **1kg (2lb) ripe plum tomatoes** and plunge them into **boiling water** for a couple of minutes. Drain the tomatoes in a colander, transfer them to a bowl of **iced water**, then drain again and remove the skins. Halve and deseed, then cut into quarters.

Meanwhile, heat **3 tablespoons olive oil** in a large saucepan over medium heat and sauté **4 garlic cloves, peeled and thinly sliced**, **2 tablespoons flat-leaf parsley, finely chopped** and **2 fresh bay leaves** for a few minutes or until softened. Add **1 teaspoon ground cinnamon** and **2 tablespoons sugar**, then cook for a further 2 minutes. Add the prepared tomatoes and cook over a low heat for 20 minutes, stirring carefully, until the mixture reduces and thickens.

Place **12 large prawns (shrimps), cleaned, deveined and with tails left on**, on top of the tomato mixture, cover with a lid, and cook for about 10 minutes, or until the prawns are cooked. Stir the mixture to coat the prawns in the sauce and serve with a **squeeze of lemon juice**, **couscous (see page 281)** or **bread**.

Beef & Cardoon Tagine

You can also make this with lamb or veal. If you can't find cardoons, substitute them with artichokes or celery.

Heat the olive oil in a casserole dish, or tagine, over a medium heat, then add the beef and brown for 5–7 minutes. Transfer beef to a plate.

Add the onions, garlic and celery to the casserole and soften for 5–7 minutes. Add the ras el hanout, cumin, ginger, saffron, turmeric, tomato purée, coriander and parsley, then cook for 5 more minutes. Season generously with salt and pepper. Return the beef to the casserole dish and add enough water to just cover the mixture. Bring to the boil, then lower the heat, cover, and simmer for 2 hours or until the meat is tender and the sauce has thickened.

Meanwhile, add half a lemon to a large bowl of cold water. Remove the tough outer stalks of the cardoons, separate the stalks and wash in cold water. Remove the strings from stalks with a sharp knife or potato peeler, placing the stalks immediately into the bowl of cold water to stop the cardoons from discolouring.

Bring a large saucepan of water to the boil over medium heat. Cut the cardoon stalks into 6cm (2⅓in) pieces and add to the boiling water. Bring the water back to the boil, then lower the heat and simmer for 10–15 minutes, or until the cardoon stalks are almost cooked. Drain then stir into the beef tagine and add with the remaining lemon halves and the olives during last 40 minutes of cooking.

Serve immediately with couscous.

Serves 6

- 2 tablespoons extra-virgin olive oil
- 1.5kg (3lb) stewing beef, such as topside or chuck, cut into 5cm (2in) pieces
- 1 large onion, peeled and sliced
- 2 garlic cloves, sliced
- 1 celery heart, trimmed and chopped
- ½ teaspoon ras el hanout (see page 258)
- 1 teaspoon ground cumin
- 1 teaspoon ground ginger
- ½ teaspoon ground saffron
- 1 teaspoon turmeric
- 1 tablespoon tomato purée
- 1 tablespoon fresh coriander (cilantro), roughly chopped
- 1 tablespoon flat-leaf parsley, roughly chopped
- sea salt
- freshly ground black pepper
- cold water
- 2 lemons, halved
- 1.5kg (3lb) cardoons
- 200g (7oz/1⅓ cup) purple olives, drained and pitted

To serve
- couscous (see page 281)

Make your own Couscous. See page 281.

Beef & Quince Tagine

Serves 6
- 2 tablespoons extra-virgin olive oil
- 1.5kg (3lb) stewing beef, such as topside or chuck, cut into 5cm (2in) pieces
- 1 large onion, peeled and sliced
- 2 garlic cloves, sliced
- 1 celery heart, trimmed and chopped
- 1 teaspoon cayenne pepper
- 1 teaspoon ras el hanout (see page 258)
- 1 teaspoon ground cumin
- 1 teaspoon ground ginger
- 1 teaspoon ground allspice
- 1 tablespoon tomato purée
- 1 tablespoon fresh coriander (cilantro), roughly chopped
- 1 tablespoon flat-leaf parsley, roughly chopped
- sea salt
- freshly ground black pepper
- cold water
- juice of 1 lemon
- 5 small quinces

To serve
- couscous (see page 281)

You can also make this with lamb or veal.

Heat the olive oil in a casserole dish, or tagine, over a medium heat, then add the beef and brown for about 5–7 minutes. Transfer the the beef to a plate.

Add the onions, garlic and celery to the casserole dish and soften for 5–7 minutes, then add the cayenne pepper, ras el hanout, cumin, ginger, allspice, tomato purée, coriander and parsley and cook for 5 more minutes. Season generously with salt and pepper.

Return the beef to the casserole dish and add enough water to just cover the mixture. Bring to the boil, then lower the heat, cover and simmer for 2 hours, or until the meat is tender and the sauce has thickened.

Meanwhile, add the juice of one lemon to a large bowl of cold water. Peel, core and slice each quince into eighths and place immediately in the bowl of cold water to stop the quince from discolouring.

Bring a large saucepan of water to the boil over medium heat. Add the quince, lower the heat and simmer for 20 minutes, or until the quince are almost cooked. Drain, then stir into the beef tagine during the last 50 minutes of cooking.

Serve immediately with couscous.

623

WILAYA DE MARRAKECH

Lamb, Potato, Broad Bean & Pea Tagine

Heat the olive oil in a casserole dish or tagine over a medium heat, add the lamb and brown for 5–7 minutes. Transfer the lamb to a plate.

Add onion, garlic and tomato to the casserole dish and soften for 5–7 minutes, then add the ginger, saffron, coriander and mint and cook for 5 more minutes. Season generously with salt and pepper.

Return the lamb to the casserole dish and add enough water to just cover the mixture. Bring to the boil, then lower the heat and simmer, covered, for 1½ hours, or until the meat is tender and the sauce has thickened. Add the potatoes, broad beans and peas during last 20 minutes of cooking.

Serve with a dollop of yoghurt and harissa on top, sprinkle with whole mint leaves and with couscous on the side.

Serves 4
- 4 tablespoons extra-virgin olive oil
- 1kg (2lb) lamb, cut into 5cm (2in) chunks
- 1 onion, peeled and chopped
- 2 cloves garlic, crushed
- 1 large tomato, peeled and chopped
- 1 teaspoon ground ginger
- 1 teaspoon saffron threads
- 1 teaspoon ground coriander (cilantro)
- 1½ tablespoons mint, finely chopped
- sea salt
- freshly ground black pepper
- cold water
- 400g (14oz) baby potatoes, cleaned
- 100g (3½oz) shelled broad beans
- 100g (3½oz) shelled fresh or frozen peas

To serve
- thick Greek-style yoghurt
- harissa (see page 267)
- whole mint leaves
- couscous (see page 281)

Couscous on the side of this dish could be great. Make your own, see page 281.

Lamb, Artichoke & Broad Bean Tagine

Serves 4

Heat **4 tablespoons olive oil** in a casserole dish or tagine over a medium heat. Add **1kg (2lb) lamb, cut into 5cm (2in) chunks** and brown for 5–7 minutes. Transfer lamb to a plate.

Add to the casserole dish **1 red onion, peeled and sliced** and **2 cloves garlic, peeled and sliced**, and soften for 5–7 minutes. Add **1 teaspoon ground ginger, 1 teaspoon saffron threads, 1 teaspoon paprika, ½ teaspoon coriander (cilantro) seeds, 1 teaspoon ground cumin, 1 tablespoon mint, roughly chopped, 1 tablespoon flat-leaf parsley, roughly chopped** and **1 tablespoon fresh coriander (cilantro), roughly chopped** and cook for 5 more minutes. Season generously with **sea salt** and **freshly ground black pepper**.

Return the lamb back to casserole dish and add enough **water** to just cover the mixture. Bring to the boil, then lower the heat, put the lid on and simmer for 1½ hours, or until the meat is tender and the sauce has thickened. Add **2 artichoke hearts, roughly chopped and cooked**, and **400g (14oz) broad beans fresh, frozen or canned**, during the last 30 minutes of cooking. Serve with **couscous** (see page 281).

Lamb & Prune Tagine

Serves 4

Heat **4 tablespoons olive oil** in a casserole dish or tagine over a medium heat, then add **1kg (2lb) lamb, cut into 5cm (2in) chunks** and brown for 5–7 minutes. Transfer the lamb to a plate.

Add to the casserole dish **1 onion, peeled and sliced, 2 cloves garlic, peeled and sliced, 1 celery stick, trimmed and chopped, 2 carrots, peeled and roughly chopped**, and **1 large tomato, peeled and chopped** and soften for 5–7 minutes. Add **1 teaspoon ground ginger, 1 teaspoon saffron threads, 1 teaspoon ground coriander (cilantro)** and **1 tablespoon flat-leaf parsley, finely chopped** and cook for 5 more minutes.

Return the lamb to the casserole dish and add enough **water** to just cover the mixture. Bring to the boil, then lower the heat, cover with the lid and simmer for 1½ hours, or until the meat is tender and the sauce has thickened. Add **300g (10½oz) pitted prunes, softened in hot water for 5 minutes**, during the last 30 minutes of cooking. Serve with **couscous** (see page 281) and sprinkled with **toasted flaked almonds**.

Find the recipe for Preserved Lemons page 253.

Saddle of Lamb, Fennel & Preserved Lemon Tagine

Heat the olive oil in a casserole dish or tagine over medium heat. Add the saddle of lamb and brown for 5–7 minutes. Transfer lamb to a plate.

Add the onions and garlic to the casserole dish and sauté for 5–7 minutes, then add the fennel and Preserved Lemons and cook for 5 minutes. Add the ginger, cumin and coriander and cook for 5 more minutes. Season generously with salt and pepper.

Return the saddle of lamb back to the casserole dish and add enough water to just cover the mixture. Bring to the boil, then lower the heat, cover with the lid and simmer for 1½ hours, or until the meat is tender and the sauce has thickened.

Serve with couscous.

Serves 4
- 4 tablespoons extra-virgin olive oil
- 650g (1lb 7oz) saddle of lamb, tied with kitchen string
- 2 medium onions, peeled and sliced
- 2 garlic cloves, peeled and thinly sliced
- 12 baby fennel, trimmed and roughly chopped
- 3 small preserved lemons, cut into quarters (see page 253)
- 1 teaspoon ground ginger
- 1 teaspoon ground cumin
- 1 teaspoon ground coriander (cilantro)
- sea salt
- freshly ground black pepper
- cold water

To serve
- couscous (see page 281)

Serves 4

- 1kg (2lb) lamb shoulder or neck, cut into 8–10cm (3–4in) pieces
- 3 baby leeks, outer leaves removed
- 5 shallots, peeled whole
- 2 carrots, peeled and chopped
- 1 ripe tomato, quartered
- 5 garlic cloves, peeled
- 1 tablespoon flat-leaf parsley, including stalks
- 1 small preserved lemon, roughly chopped (see page 253)
- 1 teaspoon saffron threads
- 1 teaspoon cumin
- 1 teaspoon paprika
- 2 tablespoons extra-virgin olive oil
- sea salt
- freshly ground black pepper
- 600ml (20fl oz/2¼ cups) cold water

To serve

- Arab-style flatbread

Lamb Tangia

You see earthenware tangia pots for sale at most butcher shops in Marrakesh. Traditionally, the butcher chops up some lamb for the pot, along with garlic cloves, salt, cumin and saffron threads. A little water and oil olive is added and then parchment paper, firmly tied with string, covers the narrow lid. The tangia is then taken to the hammam oven (*farnatchi*), used to heat the water of the hammam (wash house), and buried in hot embers for anything from five to eight hours. It's a brilliant way of cooking, traditionally used by bachelors, and only costs a few dirhams as a tip. To replicate the process, simply use an earthenware dish with a tight-fitting lid. I like to add more vegetables than they do in Morocco, which become deliciously soft and caramelised after so much slow-cooking.

Preheat the oven to 150°C (300°F). Place all the ingredients in a tangia or earthenware dish and season generously with salt and pepper. Pour in about 650ml (3 cups) water to just cover the mixture, then cover with parchment paper or foil, or top with a tight-fitting lid.

Cook in the preheated oven for 4 to 4½ hours, or until the lamb falls apart and the vegetables are tender.

Serve with flatbread.

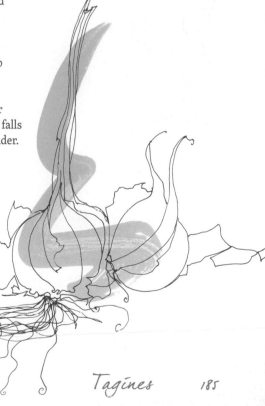

Buy your tagines
and other pottery
freshly fired from the
kiln.

Just outside Marrakesh,
The Beldi Country Club
in Cherifia is an oasis
of rose and herb gardens,
swimming pools and
artisan workshops.

Owner Jean Dominique Leymarie
and the always happy staff
are consummate hosts,
serving great food and drink
around by the swimming pools.

There are even rooms to stay in
if you need some respite
from the mayhem of the big city.

Steamed Lamb

Baba Steamed Lamb is a highlight of many Moroccan feasts, served with boiled rice and dipping sauces. It is also a simple and healthy way of cooking the meat, which is wrapped in muslin.

Serves 6

Combine **4 tablespoons extra-virgin olive oil**, **1 teaspoon saffron threads** and **1 teaspoon ground cumin** in a large bowl. Season generously with **sea salt** and **freshly ground black pepper** and mix well. Place **1.3kg (2lb 10oz) lamb shoulder** and **460g (1lb) rack of lamb** into the bowl and rub with the mixture.

Wrap lamb shoulder and rack in **a piece of muslin**, tying the muslin tightly together in a knot.

Fill the bottom part of a couscoussier three-quarters full with **cold water**, bring to the boil and then place the lamb in the top part of the couscoussier. Cover the top of the couscoussier with a damp tea towel, replace the lid and steam the lamb, undisturbed, for 2–2½ hours, or until the lamb is tender and falling off the bone.

Transfer the lamb to a chopping board. Unwrap and discard the muslin, then cut the meat into pieces. Transfer to a platter and serve immediately with **boiled rice**, **harissa** (see page 267) and **cumin salt** (see page 261) on the side.

Steamed Chicken with Rice

Serves 6

Combine **4 tablespoons extra-virgin olive oil**, **1 teaspoon saffron threads**, **1 teaspoon ground cumin**, **1 teaspoon ground cinnamon** and **½ teaspoon paprika** in a large bowl. Season generously with **sea salt** and **freshly ground black pepper** and mix well. Place **1.5kg (3lb) chicken**, **jointed into 6 pieces**, into the bowl and rub with the mixture.

Wrap the chicken pieces in **a piece of muslin**, tying the muslin tightly together in a knot.

Fill the bottom part of a couscoussier three-quarters full with **cold water**, bring to the boil and then place the chicken in the top part of the couscoussier. Cover the top with a damp tea towel, replace the lid and steam the chicken, undisturbed, for 1–1½ hours, or until the chicken is tender and falling off the bone.

Transfer the chicken to a chopping board. Unwrap and discard the muslin, then transfer to a platter or onto individual plates and serve immediately with **boiled rice**, **salad**, **harissa** (see page 267) and **cumin salt** (see page 261).

Chicken Madfoun with Vermicelli & Almonds

This is an amazing dish of melt-in-the-mouth vermicelli, chicken and almonds. If you prefer, cook the vermicelli in a saucepan of boiling salted water until cooked, drain and mix with the butter and olive oil.

Heat half the olive oil and half the butter in a casserole dish, or tagine, over a medium heat. Add the onions and sauté for 5–7 minutes until softened, then transfer to a bowl with a slotted spoon.

Add the chicken pieces to the casserole dish and sauté for 5–7 minutes until browned. Return the onions to casserole dish and add the ginger, saffron, ground cinnamon and enough water to just cover the mixture. Season generously with salt and pepper. Bring to the boil. Reduce to a low heat, cover with the lid and simmer for 1 to 1½ hours. Take the lid off and cook for a further 15 minutes, or until the chicken is tender, the onions are almost melted and the sauce has thickened.

Meanwhile, fill the bottom part of a couscoussier three-quarters full with water and bring to the boil. Add the vermicelli and cinnamon stick into the top part of the couscoussier, cover the top with a damp tea towel, replace the lid and steam for 20 minutes.

Remove from the heat and transfer the vermicelli to a large bowl. Mix in remaining olive oil and butter with your hands. Add a pinch salt and 100ml (3½fl oz) cold water and mix again. Return the vermicelli to the top part of couscoussier and steam over boiling water for a further 10 minutes.

Remove the couscoussier from the heat, discard the cinnamon stick and transfer the vermicelli to a large platter. Arrange chicken and onions on top, and spoon any remaining sauce over. Sprinkle with slivered almonds, icing sugar and cinnamon before serving.

Serves 6
- 4 tablespoons olive oil
- 80g (3oz/approx ½ stick) butter
- 3 large onions, peeled and thinly sliced
- 1 x 1.5kg (3lb) chicken, jointed into 6 pieces
- 1 teaspoon ground ginger
- 1 teaspoon saffron threads
- 1 teaspoon ground cinnamon
- cold water
- sea salt
- freshly ground black pepper
- 400g (14oz) vermicelli
- 1 cinnamon stick

To serve
- slivered toasted almonds
- icing (confectioner's) sugar
- ground cinnamon

Chicken, Preserved Lemon & Olive Tagine

Place the garlic, parsley, fresh coriander, cumin, ginger, coriander, saffron and half the olive oil in a large bowl and mix well. Add the chicken pieces and coat well with the marinade. Cover with cling film and refrigerate for a few hours or overnight.

Remove the chicken from the refrigerator. Heat the remaining oil in a large casserole dish or tagine over a medium heat, then add the onions and sauté for 5–7 minutes or until softened. Transfer the onions to a bowl with a slotted spoon and set aside. Remove the chicken pieces from the marinade to the casserole dish, and sauté for 5–7 minutes until browned. Add the softened onions, remaining marinade, lemon juice and enough water to just cover the mixture, and season generously with salt and pepper. Bring to the boil, then lower the heat and simmer for 1 hour.

Stir in the Preserved Lemon and olives and simmer, uncovered, for another 15–20 minutes, or until the chicken is tender and the sauce thickens. Serve with couscous and sprinkle with chopped flat-leaf parsley.

Serves 4–6
- 4 garlic cloves, peeled and thinly sliced
- 4 tablespoons flat-leaf parsley, finely chopped, plus extra to garnish
- 4 tablespoons fresh coriander (cilantro), finely chopped
- 1 teaspoon ground cumin
- 1 teaspoon ground ginger
- 1 teaspoon ground coriander (cilantro)
- 1 teaspoon saffron threads
- 150ml (5fl oz/⅔ cup) extra-virgin olive oil
- 1 x 1.5kg (3lb) chicken, jointed into 6 pieces
- 2 onions, peeled and sliced
- juice of 2 lemons
- sea salt
- freshly ground black pepper
- 1 preserved lemon, deseeded and roughly chopped (see page 253)
- about 20 mixed olives, drained

To serve
- couscous (see page 281)

Trid

Known as 'poor man's bisteeya', this satisfying dish can also be made with torn pieces of fried warkha pastry or grilled Arab-style flatbread (if you don't have time to make the pancakes). There is also a popular version where the pancakes are stuffed with filling.

Heat half the olive oil and butter in a casserole dish, or tagine, over a medium heat, then add the onions and garlic and sauté for 5–7 minutes until softened. Using a slotted spoon, transfer onions and garlic to a bowl.

Add the chicken pieces to the casserole dish and sauté for 5–7 minutes until browned. Return the onions and garlic to the casserole dish. Add the ginger, saffron, cinnamon, turmeric and enough water to just cover the mixture. Season with salt and pepper. Bring to the boil, then simmer, covered, over a low heat for 1 hour. Take the lid off, add lentils and cook for a further 20–30 minutes, or until the chicken and lentils are tender, onions are almost melted and the sauce thickened.

To make the pancakes, place the flour and salt into a large bowl. Make a well in the centre, add the water (or more if needed) and knead into a smooth elastic dough, folding the dough vigorously in from the sides as you knead.

Transfer to a lightly floured work surface, and continue to knead for about 15–20 minutes, or until the dough is soft and elastic. Lightly oil your hands and roll the dough in your hands until it is greased all over. Divide the dough into sixteen small balls, making sure each dough ball is well oiled. Place one of the balls on the work surface and carefully stretch and pull it out with oiled hands to make a thin pancake.

Heat a large cast iron frying pan over high heat. Carefully transfer the pancake into the pan and cook for about 2–3 minutes, turning the pancake once, or until it begins to blister and brown.

To serve, place the pancakes on a large platter, roughly tearing them a little with your hands. Place the chicken mixture on top, spooning any extra sauce over, and sprinkle with mint and coriander if desired.

Serves 6
- 2 tablespoons olive oil
- 2 tablespoons butter
- 2 large onions, thinly sliced
- 2 garlic cloves, thinly sliced
- 1 x 1.5kg (3lb) chicken, jointed into 6 pieces
- 1 teaspoon ground ginger
- 1 teaspoon saffron threads
- 1 teaspoon ground cinnamon
- 1 teaspoon ground turmeric
- cold water
- sea salt
- freshly ground black pepper
- 150g (5oz) lentils

Pancakes
- 450g (1lb/3 cups) plain (all-purpose) flour
- 1 teaspoon sea salt
- 300ml (10fl oz/1¼ cup) lukewarm water
- olive oil, for frying

To serve
- fresh mint, roughly chopped
- fresh coriander (cilantro), roughly chopped

Chicken Mefenned with Parsley Omelettes

Serves 6–8
- 1 x 1.5kg (3lb) chicken
- 1 preserved lemon (see page 253)
- 1 large onion, sliced
- 2 garlic cloves, thinly sliced
- 1 teaspoon ground ginger
- 1 teaspoon ground cumin
- 1 teaspoon saffron threads
- 3 tablespoons extra-virgin olive oil
- sea salt
- freshly ground black pepper
- cold water
- 3 tablespoons butter

Parsley Omelettes
- 10 eggs
- sea salt
- freshly ground black pepper
- ½ teaspoon ground cumin
- ¼ teaspoon paprika
- 5 tablespoons flat-leaf parsley, finely chopped
- 1 tablespoon extra-virgin olive oil

This is a gloriously sensual and somewhat messy dish, as you tear the chicken with your fingers, then wrap the bits of meat in the omelettes, which you dip in the thick sauce. Place finger bowls on the table for your guests.

Stuff the chicken cavity with a preserved lemon, then place the chicken in an oval Le Creuset-style cast iron casserole dish or saucepan. You want the chicken to fit snugly. Add the onion, garlic, ginger, cumin, saffron and 1 tablespoon of the olive oil and season generously with salt pepper. Add about 700ml (23fl oz/ 3 cups))water to just cover the chicken, then bring to the boil over a medium heat. Cover the casserole dish, reduce the heat and simmer for 1¼–1½ hours. Transfer the chicken to a plate and reserve the sauce.

Preheat the oven to 150°C (300°F). Heat the remaining olive oil and the butter in a large frying pan over medium heat, then add the chicken and brown, turning frequently so that the skin browns on all sides, for about 7–8 minutes. Transfer to a platter, cover with aluminium foil and keep warm in the preheated oven.

Meanwhile, heat remaining sauce in the casserole dish over medium heat for about 15 minutes, or until it is reduced to a thick consistency.

To make omelettes, crack the eggs in a bowl, season generously with salt and pepper and beat well. Add the cumin, paprika and parsley and beat again. Heat the olive oil in a small non-stick frying pan over high heat, add enough omelette mix to just cover the bottom of the pan and cook for a few minutes until the eggs set. Turn out onto a plate. Repeat with remaining egg mix until you've made eight thin omelettes.

To serve, place the chicken on a platter and spoon some of the sauce over the top. Cover the chicken with the omelettes. Pour the remaining sauce into a small bowl. Place a finger bowl on the table to wash hands after eating.

Roasts

Using the herbs and spices that give flavour to tagines and grills, you can add some surprisingly vibrant flavours to your regular roasts. Simply grind up spices such as ginger, cumin and coriander and combine with chopped garlic and herbs to smear as a dry-rub marinade on beef, lamb or fish before slow-roasting in the oven for some really authentic Moroccan tastes.

Roast Quail with Herb Tabbouli

If you prefer use barley couscous instead of bulghur wheat, use the same method as in the Seared Beef & Barley Couscous Salad recipe (see page 108).

Place the bulghur wheat in a large bowl, cover with water and set aside for a 1–2 hours.

To make the marinade, place all the ingredients in a bowl large enough to hold the quails. Season generously with salt and pepper, and mix until well combined.

Place the quail in the marinade and toss until they are well coated. Cover with cling film and refrigerate for at least 1 hour.

Preheat the oven to 200°C (400°F). Remove the quail from the refrigerator and place in a small roasting tin. Pour over marinade and roast in the oven for 40 minutes until golden, basting occasionally with the marinade sauce in the bottom of the roasting tin.

Meanwhile, to make Herb Tabbouli, drain the bulghur wheat in a colander, then place in a tea towel and squeeze out any excess water. Tip the bulghur into a large bowl, add the spring onions, mint, coriander, parsley, rocket, olive oil and lemon juice. Season with salt and pepper and combine.

Transfer the quails to a large serving platter, drizzle with any remaining marinade from the roasting tin, then add the Herb Tabbouli to the platter and serve immediately.

Serves 4–6
- 6 quails

Herb Tabbouli
- 200g (7oz) bulghur wheat
- cold water
- 1 bunch spring onions, including green tops, finely chopped
- 1 bunch fresh mint, including stalks, finely chopped
- 1 bunch fresh coriander (cilantro), including stalks, finely chopped
- 1 bunch fresh flat-leaf parsley, including stalks, finely chopped
- 1 small handful rocket (arugula) leaves
- 180ml (6fl oz/¾ cup) extra-virgin olive oil
- juice of 3 lemons
- sea salt
- freshly ground black pepper

Marinade
- 6 tablespoons extra-virgin olive oil
- 4 tablespoons pomegranate molasses
- 1 tablespoon coriander (cilantro) seeds
- 1 tablespoon ground cumin
- 1 tablespoon ground ginger
- 1 teaspoon saffron threads
- sea salt
- freshly ground black pepper

Roast Stuffed Fish

I first tasted this speciality from Fez at the Al Fassia – a restaurant run by women with some of the best food in Marrakesh. The vermicelli and prawn stuffing is unusual and delicious.

Preheat the oven to 180°C (350°F). Place the vermicelli in a large bowl, then add the prawns, courgettes, tomatoes, onion, celery, parsley, preserved lemon, ginger, cumin, paprika and harissa. Season generously with salt and pepper, then mix well with your hands.

Place the fish on a chopping board and score the skin three times with a sharp knife. Sprinkle with a little sea salt, ginger, cumin, paprika and harissa, and drizzle over half the olive oil. Rub the spices and oil into the cut skin, then turn over the fish and repeat the process. Repeat with the second fish.

Spoon half the vermicelli filling into a large baking tray. Place the prepared fish on top and stuff the cavities with the remaining filling. Drizzle with the rest of the olive oil and roast in the oven for about 25 minutes, or until the fish are cooked and the skin is crisp.

Transfer the stuffed fish to a platter and serve immediately.

Serves 4
- 160g (5½oz) vermicelli, cooked
- 200g (7oz) raw prawns (shrimps), peeled
- 2 courgettes (zucchinis), coarsely grated
- 3 tomatoes, peeled, deseeded and roughly chopped
- 1 small red onion, finely chopped
- 1 small celery stalk, trimmed and finely chopped
- 6 tablespoons flat-leaf parsley including stalks, roughly chopped
- 1 small preserved lemon (see page 253), finely chopped
- 1 teaspoon ground ginger, plus extra for sprinkling
- 1 teaspoon ground cumin, plus extra for sprinkling
- 1 teaspoon paprika, plus extra for sprinkling
- ½ tablespoon harissa, plus extra for sprinkling (see page 267)
- sea salt
- freshly ground black pepper
- 2 (about 350–400g/12–14oz) snapper or other large fish such as sea bream or sea bass, scaled, cleaned, fins cut off and cavity cut open
- 2 tablespoons extra virgin olive oil

Berbers

Freshly picked and salted olives

bubbling kefta and egg tagines

takeaway sheep

Bracelets and charms

pressed olive oil

Jostling through the crowds at the Sunday Berber market in Sidi Abdallah Ghiat is not for the faint-hearted. There are sheep just down from the Atlas Mountains to negotiate your way around, huge mounds of sea salt and olives, every kind of vegetable in muddy piles from the nearby fields and not a tourist trinket in sight.

Tambourines
tarijas drums

hot sauces
cooked kebabs

Mounds of red onions and fresh herbs...

Gnaoua guitars
tarpaulin shadows

There's an area underneath a tarpaulin roof where the butcher's slaughter goats and sheep or carve kilos of ruby red beef off carcasses hanging from battered brass hooks. You buy meat to take to grill stalls, located through a haze of smoke at the other end of the market. Here, they deftly cut the meat into cubes for the skewers that they then grill and serve with blackened vegetables, bread and hot sauces. Berber musicians wander around the tables as you eat, playing for a few dirhams.

Roast Spiced Beef with French Fries

Serves 6
- 1.5kg (3lb) rolled joint of beef, such as topside or sirloin, tied with kitchen string
- 1 tablespoon extra-virgin olive oil

Marinade
- 1 tablespoon paprika
- 1 tablespoon ground cumin
- 1 tablespoon fennel seeds
- 1 tablespoon ground coriander (cilantro)
- ½ tablespoon ground cinnamon
- 1 tablespoon brown sugar
- sea salt
- freshly ground black pepper

French Fries
- peanut oil, for deep-frying
- 500g (1lb) potatoes, peeled and cut into ½cm (⅛in) thick pieces and placed in bowl of cold water

To serve
- mixed green salad
- Dijon mustard

As a legacy of the French occupation of Morocco, you can still find great baguettes, French fries and decent roasting beef in the butcher shops.

Preheat the oven to 240°C (465°F).

Place all the marinade ingredients in a bowl, season generously with salt and pepper and mix well. Rub the beef all over with the marinade, place in a large bowl, cover with cling film and refrigerate for at least 1–2 hours.

Remove the beef from the refrigerator and allow to come to room temperature. Transfer the beef to a roasting tin and smear any extra marinade on top. Drizzle with olive oil and then roast in the oven for 20 minutes. Turn the oven temperature down to 180°C (350°F) and roast for a further 45 minutes for rare meat, or longer if you like your meat medium to well done.

Remove from the oven and rest, covered with foil, for 15 minutes.

Meanwhile, heat peanut oil in a deep-fryer or large saucepan to 140–150°C (275–300°F). Drain the prepared potatoes and pat dry with kitchen paper, then deep-fry for 6 minutes or until cooked through. Drain the French Fries on kitchen paper and then transfer to a large serving platter with the roast beef.

Serve with a mixed green salad and Dijon mustard.

Mechoui Lamb with Crushed Roast Potatoes & Tomatoes

Mechoui Lamb is both a celebratory dish at Moroccan feasts and an everyday way of slow-cooking lamb. In Marrakesh, just behind the Djemaa el Fna square, there's a tiny alley with three shops selling Mechoui Lamb by weight. Ovens underneath the shop floors slow-cook the lambs splayed on wooden poles. They are then hoicked out with a hook and placed on a well-worn chopping board. It's served with bread and cumin salt.

For the Smen Paste, place all ingredients in a food processor. Season generously with salt and pepper and blend to a fine paste. Transfer to a bowl.

Slash the lamb shoulders with a sharp knife and then rub the Smen Paste all over the lamb. Place the lamb in a large bowl, cover with cling film and refrigerate for at least 2 hours.

Meanwhile, par-boil the potatoes in a saucepan of salted, boiling water. Drain and roughly crush with a fork. Combine the crushed potatoes, tomatoes and olives in a bowl. Season generously with sea salt and drizzle with the olive oil.

Remove the lamb shoulders from the refrigerator and allow to come to room temperature. Preheat the oven to 220°C (430°F). Transfer the lamb and any remaining Smen Paste to a roasting tin, pour about 200ml water around the lamb and roast in the preheated oven for 20 minutes.

Turn the oven temperature down to 180°C (350°F) and roast for 3 more hours, basting occasionally with the juices in the pan, until the meat is tender and the skin is crisp and brown and can be removed easily with your fingers. Scatter the crushed potatoes, tomatoes and olives around the lamb 45 minutes before you take it out of the oven.

Remove the lamb from the oven and rest, covered with foil, for 15 minutes. Serve with the Crushed Roast Potatoes and Tomatoes, which have been kept warm in the oven, cumin salt and a sprinkle of mint.

Serves 6–8
- 2 x 1.5kg (3lb) lamb shoulders/legs
- 220ml (7½fl oz) cold water

Smen Paste
- 6 garlic cloves, roughly chopped
- 50g (2oz) fresh root ginger, peeled and chopped
- 1 tablespoon ground ginger
- 1 tablespoon ground cumin
- 1 tablespoon ground coriander (cilantro)
- 2 teaspoons chilli powder
- 2 teaspoons paprika
- ½ bunch fresh coriander (cilantro), roughly chopped
- ½ bunch flat-leaf parsley, roughly chopped
- 100g (3½oz/approx ¾ stick) butter, softened
- sea salt
- freshly ground black pepper

Crushed Roast Potatoes and Tomatoes
- 1kg (2lb) baby potatoes
- 5 tomatoes, some halved and some quartered
- 200g (7oz/1⅓ cups) black olives, pitted
- sea salt
- 2 tablespoons extra-virgin olive oil, for drizzling

To serve
- cumin salt (see page 261)
- fresh mint leaves, chopped

Roasted Lamb Shoulder with Orange & Honey Syrup

Serves 4
Preheat the oven to 240°C (465°F).

To make the Orange & Honey Syrup, place **150g (5oz/ ⅔ cup) sugar** and **100ml (3fl oz/approx ½ cup) cold water** in a small saucepan over low heat and simmer until the sugar dissolves. Add the **juice of 2 oranges** and **3 tablespoons clear runny honey**, and continue to cook for 20 minutes until you have a syrupy mixture.

Slash **1kg (2lb) lamb shoulder** with a sharp knife and season with **sea salt** and **freshly ground black pepper**. Place the lamb in a roasting tin, then brush with the Orange & Honey Syrup. Pour more syrup over the lamb and roast in the oven for 20 minutes. Turn the oven temperature down to 160°C (320°F) and roast for a further 2 hours, basting frequently with the syrup, until the lamb is falling off the bone and the skin is crisp.

Serve with **couscous** (see page 281) or **plain boiled rice**.

Mechoui-style Roast Chicken

Serves 6
For the Smen Paste, place **6 garlic cloves, chopped, 60g (2oz) ginger, peeled and chopped, ½ bunch coriander (cilantro), chopped, ½ bunch parsley, chopped, 2 tablespoons ground cumin, 2 tablespoons paprika, 2 tablespoons ground coriander (cilantro), 100g (3½oz) butter, softened,** in a food processor. Season with **sea salt** and **freshly ground black pepper** and blend to a fine paste. Transfer to a bowl. Rub the Smen Paste all over the chicken, then transfer the chicken to a large bowl, cover with cling film and refrigerate for at least 2 hours.

Remove **1.6kg (3lb 5oz) chicken, jointed into 6 pieces**, from the refrigerator and allow to come to room temperature.

Preheat the oven to 220°C (430°F). Transfer the chicken and any remaining Smen Paste to a large baking tin, pour **500ml (2 cups) cold water** around the chicken and roast in the oven for 20 minutes. Turn the temperature down to 160°C (320°F) and roast for about 2 hours more, basting occasionally with the juices in the pan, or until the meat is tender and the skin is crisp, and can be removed easily.

Serve with a **green salad** and **Za'atar Yoghurt Dressing**.

To make your own Za'atar Yoghurt Dressing mix together in a small bowl 1 tablespoon za'atar 6 tablespoons thick Greek-style yoghurt, and 2 tablespoons extra-virgin olive oil.

Desserts

Most meals in Morocco end simply with a platter of fruit, some dates or nuts. In common with many other Arab and Mediterranean nations though, it's also the custom to bring boxes of exquisite honeyed nut pastries, such as the famous Gazelle's Horns filled with orange flower-scented almond paste, as gifts when visiting a Moroccan home.

Stuffed Dates

Combine the ground almonds and lemon zest in a bowl. Place the sugar and water in a saucepan over a medium heat and stir for 2–3 minutes. When the sugar dissolves, add the butter, rose water and almond mixture and cook for about 2 minutes. Stir continuously until the mixture pulls away from the sides of the pan. Transfer to a bowl and allow to cool.

Spread some extra sugar on a large plate. Stuff a date with a slightly heaped teaspoon of the almond mixture, then carefully roll the date in the extra sugar. Repeat with remaining dates and mixture.

Using a sharp knife make 4–5 slashes on the top of the dates, then transfer to a serving plate.

Serves 6
- 300g (10½oz/2½ cups) ground almonds (almond meal)
- zest of 1 lemon
- 100g (3½oz/approx ½ cup) caster (superfine) sugar, plus extra for coating dates
- 150ml (5fl oz/⅔ cup) cold water
- 1 tablespoon unsalted butter
- 2 tablespoons rose water
- 500g (1lb 2oz – about 24) large dates, pitted and slit open lengthways

Chebakia

Traditionally, these honeyed pastries are served during the festival of Ramadan.

Place the yeast, sugar and salt in a bowl with the water. Mix well and leave in a warm place for 15 minutes. Cover with cling film and leave in a warm place for a further 45 minutes, until the mixture forms bubbles on the surface and has increased in volume.

Place the saffron in a small bowl with 2 tablespoons warm water. Mix the melted butter and olive oil in another bowl. In a large bowl, whisk the eggs with orange flower water and vinegar. Add the saffron liquid and butter-oil mixture and whisk again.

Place the flour in a large bowl. Add the egg mixture and mix with your hands, stirring constantly, until well combined. Add the yeast mixture and mix again until the dough is well combined. Turn out onto a lightly floured board and continue to knead the dough for about 10 minutes, until it is smooth and elastic, adding an extra splash of orange flower water if the mixture is too dry.

Divide the dough into six pieces. Roll out one of the dough pieces on a lightly floured surface to an approximately 40cm (16in) square then cut it into six 10cm (4in) squares. Using a pastry wheel, or a knife, cut each square into five ribbons, but not all the way to the end – make sure that you leave a 1cm (½in) strip of pastry uncut at the top end of the square. Place the five ribbons together and roll up tightly, pinching the uncut pastry up at the end with your fingers. Don't worry if it seems a messy and complicated process – the idea is to get them slightly braided and bunched together when they cook. Transfer the uncooked Chebakia to a tray and cover with a cloth. Repeat the process with the remaining dough.

Meanwhile, heat the honey over a low heat in a saucepan. Put the vegetable oil in a large saucepan to one-third full and heat to 180°C (350°F). Carefully lower the pastries in batches into the oil and cook for 1–2 minutes or until golden brown. Remove with a slotted spoon, drain on kitchen paper and place them in the saucepan of warmed honey. Transfer the Chebakia with a slotted spoon to a wire rack, sprinkle with sesame seeds and allow to cool before serving.

Serves 6–8
(makes 30 Chebakia)

- 15g (½oz) dried yeast
- 1 tablespoon granulated sugar
- pinch of salt
- 100ml (3½fl oz/½ cup) warm water, plus 2 tablespoons extra
- 1 teaspoon powdered saffron
- 100g (3½oz) unsalted butter, melted
- 60ml (2fl oz/¼ cup) extra-virgin olive oil
- 2 eggs
- 150ml (5fl oz/⅔ cup) orange flower water
- 3 tablespoons white wine vinegar
- 1kg (2lb 3oz/6½ cups) plain (all-purpose) flour
- 800ml (27fl oz/approx 3 cups) clear runny honey
- vegetable oil, for frying
- 150g (5oz/approx 1 cup) sesame seeds, toasted (optional)

Serves 8–10
(makes 36 Gazelle's Horns)

- 500g (1lb 2oz/3⅓ cups) plain (all-purpose) flour
- pinch of salt
- 4 tablespoons melted unsalted butter
- 2 tablespoons orange flower water
- 2 egg yolks, beaten
- cold water
- vegetable oil

Almond Paste Filling
- 450g (1lb) blanched almonds
- 300g (10½oz/1¼ cups) caster (superfine) sugar
- 150g (5oz) unsalted butter, melted
- 4 tablespoons orange flower water
- 1 teaspoon almond essence
- ½ teaspoon ground mastic

To serve
- icing (confectioner's) sugar, to dust

Gazelle's Horns

To make the filling, place the almonds and sugar in a food processor and blend until ground. Add the butter, orange flower water, almond essence and mastic and blend again until combined. Transfer the filling to a board and carefully roll into 36 small balls in the palm of your hands, then let stand for 30 minutes.

Meanwhile, make the pastry by placing the flour and salt in a large bowl. Make a well in the middle and slowly add the butter, orange flower water, egg yolks and 100ml (3½fl oz) cold water and mix until well combined. Turn out onto a lightly floured board and knead the dough for about 10 minutes until it is smooth and elastic.

Preheat the oven to 180°C (350°F) and lightly oil two baking trays. Carefully roll each ball of almond paste filling in the palm of your hands into a cigar shape about 4cm (1½in) long. Divide the pastry dough into 36 balls. Roll each pastry ball out on a lightly floured surface to a 12–14cm (5–5½in) circle and place a piece of filling on one half of the pastry. Fold the other half of pastry over the filling, pressing the pastry edges down with fingertips to seal, and carefully bend the pastry into a crescent shape.

Trim any excess pastry with a fluted pastry cutter and place each crescent on a baking tray. Prick each pastry 2–3 times to allow steam to escape while baking.

Bake in the oven for 20–25 minutes or until a light golden colour. Allow to cool on a wire rack before serving, dusting with icing sugar if desired.

Gueliz is home to some of the city's finest patisseries filled with all types of Moroccan favourites as well as classics from the French repertoire. There are glorious honeyed biscuits and fried warkha pastries in all shapes and sizes, almond and pistachio paste sweets, chocolate-coated cornets and shredded pastry balls, chocolate cakes and custard filled millefeuille and éclairs.

Gazelle's horns

chebbakia

honey

Almonds

tabas pastries

m'hanncha

Fekkas

amlou paste

ghoriba

Stuffed dates

walnuts

pistachios

Mint Tea Jelly

Serves 4

- 20g (¾oz) gelatine
  (or enough to give 800ml/27fl oz/
  approx 3 cups liquid a firm set,
  according to packet instructions)
- 300ml (10 fl oz/1¼ cups) cold
  water
- 2 mint tea bags
- 1 bunch fresh mint
- 500ml (17fl oz/2 cups) boiling
  water
- 20g (¾oz) caster (superfine)
  sugar

To serve
- extra mint leaves

Sprinkle the gelatine over cold water in a saucepan. Stir over a low heat until it dissolves – do not let it boil. Place mint tea bags and the mint in a large teapot and add the boiling water. Leave to infuse for 15 minutes then strain tea into a jug. Stir in the caster sugar then add to the gelatine mixture. Pour into a 20cm (8in) square baking dish and refrigerate until set, about 4 hours.

To serve, cut mint jelly into small cubes and spoon into glasses or bowls and then garnish with mint sprigs.

Orange Jelly

Serves 4

Sprinkle **20g (¾oz) gelatine** over **100ml (3½fl oz/½ cup)
water** in a saucepan. Stir over a low heat until it
dissolves – do not let it boil. Add **500ml (17fl oz/2 cups)
fresh orange juice**, **2 tablespoons orange blossom water**
and **1 tablespoon caster (superfine) sugar** and stir
well. Lightly oil **six 100ml (½fl oz) jelly moulds** and
refrigerate for 4 hours, until set.

When you're ready to serve the jellies, fill a large bowl
with boiling water. Briefly plunge the jelly moulds in for
a few seconds, making sure only the sides are immersed,
then turn the jelly moulds out onto a platter. Add **orange
segments** and drizzle with **date syrup or honey**.
Alternatively, serve on individual plates.

Pomegranate Jelly

Serves 4

Sprinkle **20g (¾oz) gelatine** over **100ml (3½fl oz/½ cup)
water** in a saucepan. Stir over a low heat until it dissolves
– do not let it boil. Add **500ml (17fl oz/2 cups) pomegranate
juice** and **1 tablespoon caster (superfine) sugar**, stirring
well so the sugar dissolves. Lightly oil **a 600ml (20fl oz
/2¼ cup) jelly mould**, then pour in the pomegranate
mixture and refrigerate for 4 hours or until set.

When you're ready to serve the jelly, fill a large bowl with
boiling water. Briefly plunge the jelly mould in for a few
seconds, making sure only its sides are immersed, then
place a plate on top of jelly mould and invert, shaking,
so the jelly comes out of the mould. Sprinkle with
pomegranate seeds and serve.

Muhallabia (Milk Pudding)

In a saucepan, mix the cornflour to a paste with some of the milk. Add remaining milk, sugar and mastic and stir mixture well. Bring to the boil slowly, stirring occasionally. Lower the heat and simmer for about 2 minutes or until mixture thickens.

Add rose water and half the almonds and cook for a few more minutes, then take off heat and transfer mixture to six 150ml (5fl oz/⅔ cup) capacity glass cups or bowls and refrigerate until chilled.

To serve, remove from the refrigerator, sprinkle with the remaining almonds and ground cinnamon.

Serves 6
- 70g (2½oz) cornflour (cornstarch)
- 500ml (17fl oz/2 cups) milk
- 100g (3½oz/½ cup) caster (superfine) sugar
- ½ teaspoon mastic, pounded
- 50ml (2fl oz/¼ cup) rose water
- 50g (2oz) blanched almonds, chopped
- 1 tablespoon ground cinnamon

Moroccan Fruit Salad with Lemon Verbena Iced Syrup

You can choose any seasonal fruits you like to make this refreshing dessert.

To make the Lemon Verbena Iced Syrup, boil the water in a saucepan. Add the sugar and fresh or dried lemon verbena and stir. Allow the mixture to cool and infuse, for at least 20 minutes. Transfer cooled syrup into ice cube trays, add flower petals and freeze into ice cubes.

Combine melon, plums cherries and figs in a large bowl, add Lemon Verbena Iced Syrup and serve.

Serves 4-6
- 1 melon, deseeded, rind removed and flesh thinly sliced
- 500g (1lb 2oz) mixed ripe plums, halved and stoned
- 125g (4oz) cherries, halved and stoned
- 4 ripe figs, quartered

Lemon Verbena Iced Syrup
- 1 litre (32fl oz/4 cups) water
- 2 tablespoons caster (superfine) sugar
- small bunch fresh lemon verbena, leaves picked, or 3 tablespoons dried lemon verbena leaves
- 2 tablespoons fresh flower petals, such as rose and hibiscus

Blood Orange Granita

Serves 6

Place **300g (10½ oz/1¼ cups) caster (superfine) sugar** and **1 litre (34fl oz/4 cups) cold water** in a saucepan over a medium heat. Heat, stirring, until the sugar dissolves, for about 5–7 minutes. Add **1 fresh bay leaf** and **2 tablespoons orange flower water**. Take off the heat and allow to into infuse for 20 minutes.

Strain the syrup into a bowl, discarding the bay leaf. Add **1 litre (34fl oz/4 cups) blood orange juice** and stir well. (Please see side note below for next steps.)

Prickly Pear Granita

Serves 4

Place **150g (5oz/⅔ cup) caster (superfine) sugar** and **500ml (17fl oz/2 cups) cold water** in a saucepan over a medium heat. Heat, stirring, until the sugar dissolves, for about 5–7 minutes, then add **1 fresh bay leaf**. Take off the heat and allow to infuse for 20 minutes.

Strain the syrup into a bowl, discarding the bay leaf. Place **16 prickly pears, peeled and chopped**, in a food processor or blender and blend until smooth. Strain into another bowl, discarding any seeds. There should be about 600ml (20fl oz) of prickly pear juice. Combine the sugar syrup and prickly pear juice, stirring well. (Please see side note below for next steps.)

Note Then transfer to a shallow metal tray and place in the freezer for about 2 hours, or until ice crystals begin to form. Scrape and stir the mixture with a fork, breaking up any icy lumps.

Continue freezing, scraping the mixture with the fork every half hour for about 3 hours, or until frozen but with a soft, grainy texture. Each granita will keep for up to 2 days in the freezer.

Watermelon Granita

Serves 4–6

Place **500g (1lb 2oz/2⅓ cups) caster (superfine) sugar** and **1 litre (34fl oz/4 cups) cold water** in a saucepan over a medium heat. Heat, stirring, until the sugar dissolves, for about 5–7 minutes. Add **5 cardamom pods, crushed, 1 fresh bay leaf** and **2 tablespoons orange flower water**. Take off the heat and allow to infuse for 20 minutes.

Strain the sugar syrup into a bowl, discarding the cardamom and bay leaf. Place **1kg (2lb 3oz) watermelon flesh, deseeded and roughly chopped** in a food processor or blender and blend until smooth. Strain to remove any remaining seeds. There should be about 1 litre (34fl oz/ 4 cups) of watermelon juice. Combine the sugar syrup and watermelon juice and stir well. (Please see side note, left, for next steps.)

Pomegranate Sorbet

Serves 4

Combine **500ml (17fl oz/2 cups) pomegranate** and the **juice of ½ a lemon** in a jug. Transfer to an ice-cream machine and freeze according to manufacturer's instructions.

Once done, either place in the freezer until ready to use or transfer immediately to serving bowls or glasses, garnishing with **pomegranate seeds**.

Blood Orange Sorbet

Serves 4

Place **500ml (17fl oz/2 cups) blood orange juice** and **1 tablespoon caster (superfine) sugar** in a jug and stir well to combine. Transfer to an ice-cream machine and freeze according to manufacturer's instructions.

Once done, either place in the freezer until ready to use or transfer immediately to serving bowls or glasses.

Serves 4-6 (makes 1 litre)
- 500ml (17fl oz/2 cups) milk
- 50ml (2fl oz/¼ cup) almond syrup
- 2 teaspoons mastic, crushed
- 6 egg yolks
- 100g (3½oz/½ cup) caster (superfine) sugar
- 1 teaspoon dried lavender flowers

To serve
- 6 ripe figs
- extra dried lavender flowers, for sprlinkling

Figs with Almond-Milk Ice Cream

Combine milk, almond syrup and mastic in a saucepan and slowly bring to the boil over a low heat, stirring occasionally to prevent burning and help the mastic dissolve.

Whisk the egg yolks and caster sugar until pale and thick, then gradually whisk in the hot milk mixture. Return to the saucepan and stir over a low heat (making sure the mixture does not boil, otherwise it will curdle) until the mixture coats the back of the spoon.

Remove from the heat and strain through a fine sieve into a bowl. Stir in lavender and allow to cool.

Refrigerate before transferring to an ice-cream maker, then freeze according to the manufacturer's instructions.

To serve, tear or cut 6 ripe figs so they're split open, then add a scoop or two of the ice cream and sprinkle with the remaining lavender.

Date Ice Cream

Place the dates, vanilla bean, double cream and milk in a saucepan and bring to a simmer over medium heat. Whisk the egg yolks in a large bowl. Slowly add the date-cream mixture then transfer to a food processor and purée until smooth. Return to the saucepan, and cook for 3 minutes over low heat, stirring constantly. Strain through a fine mesh sieve into a bowl, then chill in the refrigerator.

Freeze in an ice-cream machine according to manufacturer's instructions and use immediately, or transfer to a container and place in the freezer until ready to use.

To serve, scoop the Date Ice Cream over baklava pastries and drizzle with honey.

Serves 6–8
- 350g (12oz) dates, stoned and chopped
- 1 vanilla bean, split and scraped
- 500ml (17fl oz/2 cups) double cream
- 250ml (8½fl oz/1 cup) milk
- 6 egg yolks

To serve
- baklava pastries
- clear runny honey, for drizzling

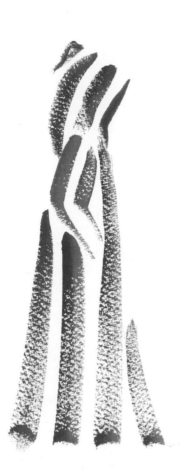

It's worth visiting
  the old Eden cinema
in the Medina's Derb Dabachi area,
  just off the Djemaa el Fna Square.

An old favourite with locals
  who come to watch Bollywood
and Kung Fu action movies,
  it's a mud-brick-walled
      architectural oddity,
  smeared with broken plate tiles
  and tattered movie posters,
  and is a really long way
    from the multiplex cinemas
    of the modern era.

The cinema even inspired
self-exiled Spanish novelist
Juan Goytisolo
as a title for his book
Cinema Eden,
Essays from the
Muslim Mediterranean.

Rice Pudding

Serves 4

Heat **600ml (20fl oz/2¼ cups) milk**, **150ml (5fl oz/⅔ cup) horchata (almond milk)** and **2 tablespoons orange zest** in a saucepan over low heat for 5 minutes. Add **200g (7oz/ 1 cup) short grain pudding rice**, **30g (1oz) caster (superfine) sugar** and **1 cinnamon stick**, bring to the boil then lower the heat and simmer for 20 minutes, adding a little more milk if the rice has absorbed all the liquid, and stirring occasionally. Stir in **2 tablespoons orange flower water** then pour into a large bowl or individual bowls and allow to cool. Serve with a **sprinkle of ground cinnamon**.

Rice Pudding Briouat

Serves 4 (makes 16)

Heat **300ml (10fl oz/1¼ cups) milk** and **100g (3½oz/ ½ cup) caster (superfine) sugar** over a low heat in a saucepan for 3–5 minutes, stirring to dissolve the sugar. Add **150g (5oz/⅔ cup) cooked short grain pudding rice**, stir well, cook for 2 minutes, then transfer to a bowl. Stir in **2 tablespoons orange flower water**, **1 tablespoon orange zest** and **1 teaspoon ground cinnamon** and leave to cool.

Take **4 sheets warkha pastry or 8 sheets filo pastry** and cut sixteen 12cm (5in) circles. Place 1 tablespoon of filling on half of the circle, and brush the edge with a little **olive oil**. Fold the pastry over to form a crescent shape, pressing down to seal. Repeat the process to make all the briouats.

Heat enough **olive oil** to come a third up the sides of a large frying pan over medium heat. When hot, carefully lower 2–3 briouats into the oil and fry, turning on all sides, until the pastry is golden brown, about 3–5 minutes. Repeat with the remaining briouats and serve immediately sprinkled with **ground cinnamon**.

Note If using filo pastry, cut into 32 circles and use 2 stacked circles of filo for each briouat, brushing with a little melted butter or olive oil between layers.

M'hanncha

Shaped like a snake from which it takes its name, this almond-filled pastry coil is easy to make once you get the hang of it. You could also add other nuts, like chopped pistachios or walnuts.

To make the filling, mix the butter, almonds, almond extract and mastic into a paste. Add the icing sugar, rose water and orange zest. Mix well then knead for a few minutes until smooth. Place mixture in a bowl and refrigerate for 15 minutes. Remove from the refrigerator and divide into ten balls. Roll each ball into a 12 x 2cm (5 x 1in) sausage shape.

Lay the warkha pastry, each sheet just overlapping the other, in a long line on a work surface. If using filo pastry, lay half the sheets down and brush with melted butter before laying the other sheets on top.

Preheat the oven to 180°C (350°F).

Spoon the filling along the bottom edge of the pastry in a line. Carefully roll the pastry up tightly into a long sausage shape, tucking in the ends to stop the filling from coming out. Brush with the melted butter.

Carefully turn the pastry roll up into a tightly coiled spiral shape. Transfer to a baking tray or metal tart dish that has been brushed with some of the melted butter.

Brush the pastry top with beaten egg and bake in the oven for 30–40 minutes, or until golden brown.

Allow to cool for 15 minutes before transferring to a plate. Dust with icing sugar and sprinkle with camomile or rose petals.

Cut into slices and serve with a dollop of Fig Jam and crème fraîche.

Serves 8–10
- 7 sheets warkha pastry or 14 sheets filo pastry
- 100g (3½oz) unsalted butter, melted
- 1 egg, beaten with a pinch of ground cinnamon
- icing (confectioner's) sugar, for dusting
- dried camomile or dried rose petals (optional), for sprinkling
- fig jam (see page 273)

Filling
- 200g (7oz) unsalted butter, at room temperature
- 360g (12oz) blanched almonds, finely ground
- ½ teaspoon almond extract
- ¼ teaspoon mastic, finely ground
- 200g (7oz/1⅓ cups) icing (confectioner's) sugar
- 4 tablespoons rose water
- zest of 1 orange

To serve
- fig jam (see page 273)
- crème fraîche

Orange Flower Doughnuts

You'll often find someone making *sfenj* (doughnuts), at Moroccan street stalls. Stallholders use oiled hands to pinch off lumps of dough, deftly making a hole in the middle of it by squeezing it between thumb and forefinger before plunging it into hot oil until golden brown. It's quite a tricky process till you get the knack and, frankly, just as easy to make hole-less doughnuts in the Greek and Italian style.

Place the warm water in a bowl with the yeast and sugar, mix well, cover with cling film and leave in a warm place for about 45 minutes, until mixture forms bubbles on surface and has increased in volume.

Place the flour and salt in a large bowl. Make a well in the centre, add the yeast mixture, orange flower water and water (add more if needed) and knead into a smooth elastic dough, folding the dough vigorously in from the sides as you knead. Keep kneading and punching the dough for about 15–20 minutes, adding a little extra water from time to time, until the dough is spongy, soft and sticks to your hands.

Place in a lightly oiled bowl, cover with a cloth and leave to rest in a warm place for 2–3 hours, until the dough has doubled in volume.

Fill a large, deep saucepan or deep fryer one-third full with vegetable oil and heat to 200°C (400°F). Very carefully fry egg-sized pieces of dough in batches, turning and making sure they are not overcrowded, until they swell in size, turn golden-brown and become crisp – about 3–5 minutes.

Remove with a slotted spoon, drain on kitchen paper, then transfer to a large plate and serve drizzled with Hibiscus Syrup or honey.

Find the recipe for Hibiscus Syrup on page 274.

Serves 4–6 (makes 18)

- 4 tablespoons warm water
- 10g (⅓oz) dry yeast
- 2 tablespoons granulated sugar
- 500g (1lb 2oz/3⅓ cups) plain (all-purpose) flour
- generous pinch of sea salt
- 1 tablespoon orange flower water
- 250ml (8½fl oz/1 cup) cold water
- vegetable oil for frying

To serve
- hibiscus syrup (see page 274) or clear runny honey, for drizzling

Condiments

Apart from the layered and abundant use of spices and herbs in Moroccan cooking, there's a widespread reliance on some fundamental prepared ingredients such as Preserved Lemons, Ras el Hanout spice mix and Harissa chilli sauce. Delicious Pickled Vegetables and Quails Eggs also add colour and flavour to many everyday dishes.

Preserved lemons are great roasted with chicken or fish, added to salad dressings and salads.

Makes enough to fill a 1 litre jar
- 10–12 lemons
- 220g (8oz) coarse sea salt
- 4 fresh bay leaves
- 2 cinnamon sticks
- cold water

Preserved Lemons

In Morocco, preserved lemons are sold both loose and in jars and in all shapes and sizes in the markets. Although you can buy preserved lemons in most good supermarkets, it's easy to make your own at home. You will need a sterilized 1 litre (34 fl oz) Kilner-style jar.

Squeeze the juice from six lemons into a bowl. With a sharp knife cut a deep cross into the top of the remaining lemons, cutting almost, but not all the way, down to the bottom of each lemon – make sure that the cut pieces are still joined at the bottom of each lemon.

Sprinkle a tablespoon of salt inside each cut lemon then push the halves back together and place carefully in the sterilized jar. Layer the remaining salt, bay leaves and cinnamon sticks in between the lemons. Pour in the lemon juice and top up with a little water. Seal tightly and leave for a month in a cool, dark place, shaking the jar every other day. After a month, they are ready to use.

Serves 6–8

- 400g (14oz) carrots, peeled and sliced
- 300g (10½oz) daikon (mooli), peeled and thinly sliced
- 400g (14oz) cucumber, peeled and thinly sliced
- 1 large red onion, peeled and thinly sliced
- 180g (6oz) sea salt
- 2 garlic cloves, peeled and thinly sliced
- rind from 1 small preserved lemon (see page 253), thinly sliced
- ½ teaspoon cumin seeds
- ½ teaspoon coriander (cilantro) seeds
- 1 cinnamon stick
- 1 tablespoon granulated sugar
- 500ml (17fl oz/2 cups) white wine vinegar
- juice of 1 lemon

Pickled Vegetables

Pickled vegetables (such as chillies, gherkins and turnips) are found throughout the Arab world and North Africa, and feature on mezze platters. Salting the vegetables first helps keep them crisp.

Place the carrot, daikon, cucumber and onion in a bowl, add salt and stir well. Leave for 30 minutes then place in a colander and carefully rinse vegetables under cold water to remove all the salt. Transfer to kitchen paper to dry, then place in a large bowl.

Add the garlic, preserved lemon rind, cumin and coriander seeds, cinnamon, sugar, vinegar and lemon juice to the vegetables. Mix well, cover with cling film. Refrigerate for at least 2 hours before serving.

Alternatively, place in a sterilized jar, seal tightly and store for up to 2 months.

Serves 6

- 24 quail eggs
- 100ml (3½fl oz/½ cup) dry white wine
- 250ml (8½fl oz/1 cup) white wine vinegar
- cold water
- 1 small red onion, peeled and thinly sliced
- ½ teaspoon cumin seeds
- 1 cinnamon stick
- 3 fresh bay leaves, roughly chopped
- 8 cloves
- ½ teaspoon black peppercorns
- ½ teaspoon coriander (cilantro) seeds
- sea salt

Pickled Quail Eggs

Bring a large saucepan of water to the boil over high heat. Carefully add the eggs and cook for 3 minutes. Drain and peel the eggs under cold running water.

Place the wine, vinegar and about 50ml (2fl oz) of cold water in a small saucepan. Add onion, cumin seeds, cinnamon stick, bay leaves, cloves, peppercorns, coriander seeds and a generous pinch of salt. Bring to the boil over medium heat then simmer over low heat for 5 minutes. Add the eggs and cook for 2 minutes, then remove the pan from the heat.

Allow to cool before transferring the eggs, pickling spices and liquid to a sterilized jar. Refrigerate until ready to use. The quail eggs will keep for about 2 weeks this way.

Serve as a snack with olives or add to salads.

Ras el Hanout

This spice blend is something that every visitor is cajoled into buying when wandering around the souks. In Morocco, it's used in game dishes, bistillas and tagines such as *mrouzia* (lamb, raisins, almonds and honey). It also flavours *majoun* (hashish, dried nuts, fruits, Smen and honey candy) or 'love potion' to give it its Arabic name, an indication of its purpose as a stimulant.

Ras el Hanout translates as 'head of the shop', each spice merchant has his own special recipe of at least fifteen, and up to thirty, different spices that usually includes nutmeg, cardamom, mace, ginger, cloves, lavender, cayenne, orris root, cinnamon, cumin seeds, turmeric, aniseed, rosebuds, allspice, coriander seeds, white peppercorns, cubeb or Java pepper, fennel seeds, cassia bark, tara soudania (earth almonds), grains of paradise, nigella seeds, wild or black cardamom, ash berries and not to mention belladonna berries, reputed aphrodisiacs such as Spanish fly (cantharides beetle) and Vitex agnus-castus (monk's pepper). The best mixes have an ethereal and lingering sensual flavour, so not much is needed to impart a potent taste to dishes.

It would be foolish to make your own version of this spice mix in Morocco as there are a great deal of merchants making excellent blends. However, as much of the commercial Ras el Hanout available in the UK is of dubious authenticity, give it a try. It's hard to give a precise recipe as there are often so many hard-to-find ingredients used, experiment with what you have until you get the flavour you like.

Combine all the ingredients in a spice blender or food processor and blend to a fine powder. Transfer to a jar and seal tightly.

Makes about 100g (3½oz)
- 8 rosebuds
- 6 cinnamon sticks
- 6 mace blades
- 2 tablespoons nutmeg
- 2 tablespoons turmeric
- 1 small piece of orris root
- 1 tablespoon lavender
- 1 tablespoon coriander (cilantro) seeds
- 1 tablespoon cumin seeds
- 1 tablespoon fennel seeds
- 1 tablespoon white peppercorns
- 2 tablespoons allspice berries
- 10 cardamom pods
- 1 small piece galangal
- 1 small piece ginger
- ½ tablespoon cayenne
- 8 cloves

Makes about 85g (3oz)
- 6 tablespoons coarse sea salt
- 6 tablespoons ground cumin

Cumin Salt

This simple seasoning is perfect for sprinkling on salads and soups or with bread and extra-virgin olive oil.

Combine the salt and cumin well and store in a container or small bowl until needed.

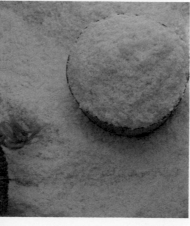

dried lizards and snakes

Argan oil

sweet cinnamon

Saffron threads

lace-like mace

Mortar and pestle

Sacks of dried fruit peel

Choose the right spice store and you're in for a real treat. The owner will sit you down with a glass of mint tea and bring out all his spice mixes and herbal cures. If he's passionate, it's less about the ultimate sale (as he knows you'll probably buy something out of guilt) and more about showing the pride in his profession. The surroundings might seem humble, but the history and lore of all its ingredients offers a fascinating insight into Moroccan cuisine and culture.

Herb Smen

Serves 6

Smen is a prized cooking oil made from clarified butter, that's then aged until it has a strong flavour. In Morocco, you can find all types of Smen in the markets. It's used in soups and tagines, and most commonly as a rub for Mechoui Lamb.

Mix **250g (9oz/2 sticks) unsalted butter, 2 tablespoons dried oregano, 2 tablespoons finely chopped dried bay leaves, 2 tablespoons dried mint** and **1 tablespoon sea salt** in a bowl until well combined then transfer to a Kilner-style jar, or other wide-mouthed jar, until ready to use. It's best to keep it as long as possible, at least a week, before using, and the mixture will keep indefinitely if stored in the fridge. The longer you keep the smen the stronger it will taste.

Amlou

Makes about 480g (1 lb 1oz)

This North African equivalent of peanut butter can be bought in pâtisseries throughout Morocco, but is even easier to make at home. It can be made either chunky or smooth, just blend the almonds accordingly. It's lovely on toast, drizzled on ice cream or stirred through yoghurt.

Place **250g (9oz) almonds** in food processor and blend to desired consistency. Transfer to a large bowl. Add **150ml (5fl oz/½ cup) argan oil** and **4 tablespoons clear runny honey** and combine mixture well. Spoon into a sterilized jar and keep for up to 2 months.

Harissa

These days Harissa sauce is widely available in tins and jars, but it's still fun to make your own. There are lots of recipe variations for this ubiquitous condiment that is found throughout North Africa. You can add different ground spices to the basic chilli-garlic mix or use fresh instead of dried chillies.

Place the chillies in a bowl, cover with warm water and leave to soak for 1 hour. Drain and transfer into a food processor. Add the garlic and salt and blend to a rough paste. Add lemon juice and olive oil then transfer to a sterilized jar.

Alternatively, roughly chop the chillies then place in a mortar and pound into a rough paste with a pestle. Add the garlic and salt and continue pounding till you have a smooth paste. Stir in the lemon juice and olive oil, then transfer into a jar.

Drizzle a little olive oil over the top and seal with a lid. Refrigerate until ready to use, or keep indefinitely in a sealed jar in the refrigerator.

Makes about 480g (17oz)
- 75g (2½oz) dried hot red chillies, deseeded
- 6 garlic cloves, peeled
- 3 tablespoons sea salt
- juice of ½ lemon
- 5 tablespoons extra-virgin olive oil, plus extra for drizzling

- 3 garlic cloves, roughly chopped
- 1 teaspoon ground cumin
- ½ teaspoon cayenne pepper
- ½ teaspoon paprika
- 1 red chilli, deseeded and sliced
- 1 teaspoon saffron
- 2 tablespoons flat-leaf parsley, roughly chopped
- 2 tablespoons fresh coriander (cilantro), roughly chopped
- sea salt
- freshly ground black pepper
- juice of ½ lemon
- 4 tablespoons extra-virgin olive oil

Chermoula

This spice mix is widely used in fish dishes and can also be used to flavour meat before grilling.

Combine the garlic, cumin, cayenne pepper, paprika, chilli, saffron, parsley and coriander (cilantro) in the bowl of a food processor. Season with salt and pepper then blend until well combined. Stir in the lemon juice and olive oil until you have a rough paste. (You could also do this with a large pestle and mortar.) Transfer to a large bowl, cover with cling film and refrigerate.

To use, smear fish or meat with Chermoula and leave for at least 20 minutes before cooking.

Serves 4

- 150g (5oz) dried figs, roughly chopped
- 300g (10½oz) pears, cored and cut into small pieces
- 1 cinnamon stick
- 2 tablespoons caster (superfine) sugar
- juice of 1 large orange
- 150ml (5fl oz/⅔ cup) cold water

Fig Jam

You can serve this for dessert with M'hanncha (see page 246) but it is also delicious with simple cold meats or cheese.

Place all the ingredients into a saucepan. Add the water and simmer over low heat, stirring occasionally and adding a little extra water if the mixture is too dry, for about 30–40 minutes until the mixture thickens to a soft and sticky consistency.

Allow to cool before using. This will keep in the fridge for up to 2 weeks.

Lemon Verbena Syrup

Makes about 850ml (29fl oz)
Place **250g (9oz/approx 1 cup) caster (superfine) sugar**
and **500ml (17fl oz/approx 2 cups) cold water** in a
saucepan over medium heat. Stir until the sugar dissolves,
about 5–7 minutes. Add **100g (3½oz) fresh lemon verbena**
and **150g (5oz) dried lemon verbena**, remove from the heat
and allow to cool and infuse for at least 20 minutes. Strain
the syrup into a bowl, discarding the lemon verbena.

Transfer to a sterilized jar and seal until ready to use.

Hibiscus Syrup

Makes about 850ml (29fl oz)
**Dried hibiscus (also known as rosella) gives the syrup
a great colour. If you can find dried orange flower
blossoms, add them as well along with dried camomile
and lemon verbena for added depth of flavour. Keep this
syrup in a sealed jar and simply spoon over fruit salads,
yoghurt and ice cream.**

Place **250g (9oz/approx 1 cup) caster (superfine) sugar**
and **600ml (20fl oz/2¼ cups) water** in a saucepan over a
medium heat. Stir, until the sugar dissolves, about
5–7 minutes. Add **120g (4oz) dried hibiscus, 2 tablespoons
dried orange flower blossoms, 2 tablespoons dried
lemon verbena, and 1 tablespoon dried camomile flowers**.
Stir in **1 tablespoon clear runny honey** then allow to cool
and infuse for at least 20 minutes. Transfer to a sterilized jar
and seal until ready to use.

If you prefer a clear syrup, strain the mixture through
a sieve into a bowl before transferring to a jar.

Pomegranate Dressing

Serves 4–6

To make the pomegranate dressing, in a mortar, pound the **pomegranate seeds from 1 pomegranate**, **1 tablespoon honey**, **3 tablespoons red wine vinegar** and **½ teaspoon ground ginger** with a pestle. Slowly add the **4 tablespoons extra-virgin olive oil**, mixing until well combined, then transfer to a bowl and set aside until ready to use. Use as a salad dressing or salsa with grilled meats.

Pomegranate & Citron Presse

Serves 2

Divide the **juice of 4 lemons, strained, 2 tablespoons fresh pomegranate seeds** and **2 teaspoons granulated sugar** between two glasses. Stir well then top up with **cold water**, to taste, adding ice cubes, if desired.

Glossary

Enter a Moroccan spice shop and you'll be
overwhelmed by the sheer variety of herbs
and spices on offer. Apart from the weird
and wonderful herbal remedies – everything
from made to order love potion vials to
bundles of dried herbs for boiling into teas
for various ailments – there are all the ground
spices that are used on a regular basis in the
country's cuisine.

Couscous

Instant couscous is widely available and just requires the addition of hot water. If you have the time, the best way to prepare couscous is still the traditional method of steaming in a couscoussier three or four times, and aerating the couscous in a bowl between each steaming.

Place the couscous in a large bowl, cover with cold water and mix well with your hands. Drain immediately and place back in the bowl, then leave for 10 minutes. Rub the grains together between your hands, letting the couscous fall back into the bowl, to break up any lumps. Leave for a further 10 minutes. Add the olive oil, a pinch of salt, and about 100ml (3½fl oz) cold water and mix well with your hands until all the liquid is absorbed.

Fill the bottom part of a couscoussier three-quarters full with water and bring to the boil. Put the couscous into the top part of the couscoussier, cover with the lid and steam for 30 minutes. Remove from the heat and transfer the couscous back into the large bowl.

Allow to cool then mix in one-third of the butter with your hands, making sure you combine it well into the couscous grains. Then, slowly add about 300ml (10fl oz) cold water with the couscous grains and combine well. Return the couscous to the top part of couscoussier, cover with the lid, and steam over the boiling water for 20 minutes.

Transfer the couscous back into the bowl, allow to cool then add another third of the butter and mix well with your hands. Return the couscous back to the top part of couscoussier and steam for another 20 minutes, or until the grains are swollen and soft. Remove the couscoussier from the heat and transfer the couscous to the bowl again. Allow to cool slightly, then add the remaining butter and mix with your hands until well combined. Transfer to a serving bowl.

Serve as an accompaniment to tagines or as a Seffa (sweet couscous, see page 10) dish.

Serves 4-6

- 500g (1lb 2oz/2½ cups) couscous
- cold water
- 2 tablespoons extra-virgin olive oil
- sea salt
- 180g (6oz/approx 1½ sticks) unsalted butter, divided into thirds

Moroccan Bread

Makes four 18cm round loaves
- 20g (¾oz) fresh yeast
- 450ml (15fl oz/approx 2 cups) warm water
- 900g (2lb/6 cups) plain (all-purpose) flour, sifted
- 100g (3½oz) fine polenta, plus extra for dusting
- 1 tablespoon salt
- 1 tablespoon extra-virgin olive oil, plus extra for brushing
- 1 tablespoon sesame seeds

These flat loaves are sold on every Moroccan street corner and are integral to every meal. They are perfect for mopping up tagine sauces or sliced in two for impromptu sandwiches.

In a small bowl, mix the yeast with a little of the warm water.

Place the flour and polenta in a large bowl. Add the salt, olive oil, yeast and remaining warm water and mix to a make a dough.

Transfer to a surface lightly dusted with flour and knead thoroughly for 15–20 minutes, punching the dough down several times while kneading, and adding a little more water if the dough is too stiff. When the dough begins to soften and become elastic, divide it into four balls.

Transfer each ball to a baking sheet, sprinkled with some polenta, and flatten the dough with the palm of your hand into an 18cm (7in) circle that is about 2cm (¾in) thick. Brush each loaf with a little extra olive oil.

Cover each loaf with a cloth and allow to rise in a warm place for about 1½ hours, or until the dough doubles in size. To check if the loaves are ready, press your thumb into one of the loaves and the dough should spring back into shape.

Preheat the oven to 200°C (400°F). Prick each loaf with a fork, and brush with a little olive oil. Sprinkle with sesame seeds and bake in the oven for 45 minutes, or until golden brown and hollow-sounding when tapped on the bottom. Transfer your loaves onto a wire rack and cool until ready to use.

Virtually every street corner
has a darkened bakery
with a cavernous wood-fired oven.

Apart from baking
the thin Moroccan round loaves
that the whole nation devours
on a daily basis, the bakers
also roast peanuts and almonds
for the local nut sellers,
and slow-roast vegetables
and meat dishes for those
families without ovens.

Serves 4
- 1½ tablespoons Chinese gunpowder or green tea
- 8 sugar cubes
- fresh mint or spearmint

Mint Tea

Mint tea is the national drink of Morocco and the ritual of offering and drinking tea is a key part of traditional hospitality. All day it is served from metal teapots, poured from a great height into small glasses and then sweetened with lashings of sugar.

Pour the tea into a glass, slowly raising the teapot to a greater height as you pour to help cool and aerate the tea.

Serve with Moroccan or Middle Eastern-style pastries.

Moroccan Spices

1. Sweet Paprika
Widely used in tagine and kefta (meatball) recipes, a pinch of paprika also enlivens many soups, sauces and salads.

2. Cumin
Kamoun is the indispensable spice of the Moroccan kitchen. It's often sprinkled over salads and brochettes and is the main ingredient for flavouring Mechoui Lamb and Chermoula spice mix.

3. Flavoured Salt
Combine common Moroccan spices with sea salt for interesting table condiments. They're perfect for salads and grilled meats.

4. Hot Paprika
Add this hotter version, *felfa harra*, if you want to turn up the heat in your marinades, sauces and kefta mixes.

5. Pepper
Black pepper is more common, mostly used ground and always added liberally early on when cooking dishes.

6. Colouring
Used as a cheaper substitute for saffron, it's only real benefit is as a colouring agent.

7. Coriander (Cilantro)
Although the fresh leaves and roots are often used as a herb or garnish, ground coriander is preferred as a frequent ingredient in tagine spice mixes and rubs.

8. Turmeric
Often rubbed onto chicken and fish kebabs, turmeric is also added to soups and tagine spice mixes.

9. Ras el Hanout
Ground mixtures of this legendary spice mix can be widely bought, you only need a pinch of the best to add real flavour to a variety of dishes.

10. Ginger
Ground *skinjbir* is used in tagines, kefta mixes and desserts to great effect. Fresh ginger is rarely used in Morocco.

11. Cinnamon
Often used liberally, ground cinnamon is dusted onto bistilla savoury pies and all manner of warkha sweet pastries. It's also sprinkled over milk and rice puddings.

12. Mrouzia Spice Mix
Mrouzia is a famed sweet lamb dish using honey, nuts and this spice mix that is similar to Ras el Hanout.

13. Salt
If you're in Morocco, use the cheap and excellent local coarse sea salt to bake whole fish in the oven, scented with herbs and spices.

14. Thyme
Dried thyme is not commonly used except in certain therapeutic soups and with grilled meat dishes.

15. Vanilla Salt
Sprinkle this interesting salt mix liberally on fresh fruit salads, sweet pastries and soups.

Moroccan Grains & Pulses

1. Couscous
Along with bread, couscous (ground semolina granules) – usually served as a de rigeur accompaniment to tagines or as a sweet dessert dish – is the staple of the Moroccan diet.

6. Lentils
Moroccans eat lentil soup almost on a daily basis and they're also great as a salad, with preserved or fresh lemon segments, herbs and chillies.

2. Rice
Rice is often found in restaurants as a side dish for grilled meats and is also used as a stuffing for vegetables.

7. Broad Beans
Dried broad beans are the prime ingredient in Bessara Soup and also make a fine dip with olive oil, cumin and paprika.

5. Split Peas
Soaked and boiled split peas make a great dip spiced with ginger and coriander and lashings of olive oil.

3. Vermicelli
Broken up vermicelli is the most popular pasta used in many soups. Nowadays, many modern, Westernized families also cook spaghetti with tomato sauce as a regular filling family meal.

4. Barley Couscous
Barley (and millet couscous) is used by many Berber households. Barley couscous, with its slightly nutty flavour and coarser texture, is great with chopped herbs in salads.

Moroccan Ingredients

1. Lemon Verbena
Lemon verbena or *verveine* is mostly used as a tea to aid digestion. The leaves also add great flavour when infused into a sugar syrup.

2. Camomile
Commonly used throughout the Arab world as a tea to help restlessness and aid sleep, you can also infuse the flowers in boiling water to use to bathe sore eyes.

3. Karkade
These dried hibiscus flowers are used throughout the Mahgreb and Arab world to make a fragrant tea said to lower the blood pressure.

4. Lavender
Known as *kzama*, dried lavender can be used sparingly in ice cream and dessert recipes or simply placed in bunches in clothes drawers.

5. Cardamom
Mostly used to flavour coffee in the Arab world, cardamom also makes its way into some pastries and desserts.

6. Rose Flowers
In Morocco, dried rose flowers and buds are mostly used in teas and sweet sauces or as a garnish to many desserts.

7. Saffron
Called *zafrane* in Morocco, every family tries to scatter a few strands of this expensive spice into meat tagines and the classic Pigeon Bistilla.

8. Oregano
Dried oregano, along with thyme, is used for slow-cooked meat dishes such as Mechoui Lamb and kebabs.

9. Sesame Seeds
Sprinkled on breads and briouats, sesame seeds are also added to cooked vegetable salads such as Caramelised Tomatoes, carrots and pumpkin.

10. Ras el Hanout
You can buy all the whole ingredients for Ras el Hanout at spice stores in Marrakesh to keep in a sealed airtight jar and use at will.

11. Poppy
Known by its French name *coquelicot*, dried poppy leaves are sometimes used as a herbal tea for headaches.

12. Cinnamon Sticks
You find whole cinnamon sticks flavouring many tagines, hot teas and spice mixes.

13. Garlic
Garlic cloves are universally peeled and chopped into marinades, sauces and stews.

14. Mint
Fresh and dried mints are used for the daily tea ritual. Dried mint and spearmint also finds their way into Herb and Goat's Cheese Briouats and flavoured Smen Butter.

15. Bay
Dried bay leaves are more commonly used in cooking, pounded in a mortar with a pestle for Chermoula and other spice mixes.

16. Cumin Seeds
Although they use ground cumin on a regular basis in Morocco, cumin seeds are also scattered onto chicken and fish dishes.

Gnaoua musicians

Scented candles

colour and movement

sensual flesh

Apart from the magnificent views of all the nightly action on the Djemaa el Fna square that can be had from Le Marrakchi (a three-floored restaurant on the corner of Rue des Banques), there's the nightly spectacle of a belly dancing floor show underneath a magnificent chandelier. Music is played by accomplished Gnaoua musicians but it's the women that steal the show.

With Love

Thank You

Thanks to all our friends in Marrakesh who
welcomed us into their homes and allowed
us to cook in their kitchens,
especially Trevor, Danny and Katrina
for all their generosity and support;

the hard-working and always smiling
Driss, Aicha, Sofia
and the two Loubna's who helped carry
our overflowing shopping baskets
back from the Mellah market
on a regular basis;

to Omar for his therapeutic pummelling
after our long shoots at the local hammam;

our stalwart fixer extraordinaire,
Tim Buxton;

Lizzie Harris and Debbie Loftus
for putting up with our constant
weekend travels to Morocco,
and late-night London writing sessions;

Sarah Tildesley
for help cooking
on one of our Marrakesh trips;

Jayne Connell, Louise Draper
and Christina Beani at Interstate
for their always passionate desire
to create this beautiful book;

and finally, Kate Pollard
and notably Julie Pinkham
at Hardie Grant for their
unwavering support of this project.

Thank You   297

Index

Page numbers in **bold** indicate
a photographic reference.